Practical English 2

second edition

Practical English 2

second edition

TIM HARRIS

Illustrated by **ALLAN ROWE**

HEINLE & HEINLE

THOMSON LEARNING

Australia Canada Mexico Singapore Spain United Kingdom United States

HEINLE & HEINLE

THOMSON LEARNING

Practical English 2/Second Edition
Tim Harris

Printed in Canada

15 16 17   06 05 04 03 02

For more information contact Heinle & Heinle, 25 Thomson Place, Boston, MA 02210 USA, or you can visit our Internet site at http://www.heinle.com

For permission to use material from this text or product contact us:

Tel:	1-800-730-2214
Fax:	1-800-730-2215
Web:	www.thomsonrights.com

ISBN: 0-15-570920-8

Library of Congress Catalog Card Number: 86-80046

Preface
to the Second Edition

Practical English has been revised and expanded, taking into account the latest developments in English language teaching. Here's what to look for in the Second Edition:

- **A more balanced approach**. The new edition gives students more opportunities to perform language functions as they learn the basic structures. They practice asking for and giving information, expressing likes and dislikes, making suggestions, agreeing and disagreeing, and so on.

- **Greater emphasis on interactive communication and personal expression**. New illustrations and exercises provide many additional opportunities for students to ask each other questions and express themselves on a variety of subjects.

- **More writing activities**. These include composition exercises designed to help students make the transition from writing sentences to writing paragraphs. Picture stories and personal questions on a given topic provide material for writing short compositions.

- **Addition of two review chapters to book 1, book 2, and book 3.** These chapters contain humorous dialogues and stories, and a variety of exercises that reinforce and expand on material presented earlier. Tests are also included to help evaluate the students' progress.

- **Introduction of a split edition**. A six-volume split edition of *Practical English* is now available in addition to the regular three-volume series. The split edition is ideal for short courses offering fewer hours of instruction.

Preface
to the First Edition

Practical English is a comprehensive series designed to teach English as a second or a foreign language. Students who use *Practical English* will learn all four language skills—listening, speaking, reading, and writing—from the beginning. In book 1 the emphasis is on oral communication; books 2 and 3 give increased attention to reading and writing. Supplementary materials include workbooks and tape cassettes for additional writing and listening practice, and instructor's manuals containing useful teaching suggestions and answers to all text and workbook exercises.

In writing *Practical English* our overriding concern has been to create material that is appropriate for adult and secondary-school students. This has been accomplished by using a broad range of characters and real-life situations to teach the language. The grammar is presented in a way that takes advantage of the greater maturity and reasoning power of students at the adult and secondary levels. Structural items are demonstrated, rather than taught in the form of rules to be memorized. Students are encouraged to form their own conclusions based on the examples given. The idea is to get the students involved in a creative learning process that enables them to develop their grammatical intuition.

There is no question that mature students need a sound working knowledge of grammar if they are to be confident and creative in using their new language. However, it is not enough to master the grammatical structures of English. Students must be able to relate the language to their own personal needs and interests. For this reason, *Practical English* includes a number of open-ended exercises that allow for free expression.

The free-response questions in the first book give students the opportunity to talk about themselves using simple, straightforward English. Once they have progressed beyond the elementary level, they are ready for more creative language practice. In books 2 and 3, each chapter has a special section called "One Step Further" with discussion topics such as sports, hobbies, music, cinema, travel, dating, and marriage. Ideas for sketches have been provided to give additional opportunities for free expression. The general themes are familiar to students, as they are drawn from the dialogues and stories in the text.

Among the outstanding features of *Practical English* are the following:

1. **Preliminary oral work**. We feel that beginning students should have the opportunity to hear and use the target language before they open their books. Direct interaction between instructor and students makes it possible to engage in meaningful communication from the first day of class. In the instructor's manual we have included detailed, easy-to-follow suggestions for introducing new structures orally, without the aid of a text. Instructors can adapt these techniques to suit their own teaching styles.

2. **Illustrated situations**. As soon as a given item has been introduced orally, students should encounter it in a situational context. This ordinarily takes the form of an illustrated situation accompanied by a short reading or story. The students are asked to describe the illustration in their own words before hearing the accompanying text. This oral activity helps students retain what they have already learned

and serves as a lead-in for the text, which has been specially written to teach the new structure. The instructor may read the text to the class or have students listen to it from a tape. Then they answer questions based on the text, while looking at the illustration. The students respond to what they see and hear without referring to a text, just as they would in actual conversation.

3. Dialogues. Each chapter in the books is divided into three units. Sections A and B generally begin with an illustrated situation featuring a basic grammatical structure. The structure appears next in a situational dialogue with pictures to help students understand the meaning of the statements. As with the illustrated situations, the dialogues may be read to the class or heard from a tape. When students have had sufficient practice in listening to a particular dialogue and repeating the statements, the instructor may ask comprehension questions based on the text. The dialogues are short and well defined, so that students can learn them quickly and act out the parts. As an alternative to acting, students may be asked to reconstruct a given dialogue by referring only to the pictures.

4. Oral exercises. The illustrated situations and dialogues are followed by oral exercises or drills, which give further practice in using the same structures. The various exercise techniques include transformation, question-and-answer, substitution, and sentence completion. The exercises are relatively simple at the beginning of each chapter, becoming more difficult toward the end. They are designed to help students acquire language concepts, as well as accuracy and fluency in speaking.

5. Reading passages. Section C of most chapters opens with an illustrated reading passage that combines new structures with previous material in a natural context. The passage is followed by a series of comprehension questions that can be done orally or in written form, in class or at home. The reading passage provides a useful context for class conversation and, in many instances, for sketches.

By the time students come to the reading passage they will generally have sufficient confidence in using the new structures to do a sketch based on the story. Acting-out situations should be encouraged whenever possible, as this gives students a chance to be spontaneous and creative in using their new language. Accordingly, the major portion of each book is given over to illustrated situations, dialogues, and reading passages, all of which promote dramatization and interaction on the part of students.

6. Review exercises. In addition to the reading passage, section C contains review exercises designed to reinforce and consolidate what has been learned in sections A and B. The exercises in section C are generally more difficult than those in sections A and B and may be assigned as homework.

Section C also has lists of new vocabulary and expressions, followed by pronunciation exercises. The pronunciation exercises focus on sounds that have proved difficult for students of English as a second or a foreign language.

7. Grammar frames. At the end of section C there are grammar frames that summarize the basic structures taught in the chapter, confirming what students have learned through concrete observation and practice. The grammar frames allow students to review at home the structural material they have been learning in class.

Students using *Practical English* will find it much easier to assimilate the basic grammar points as they encounter each item in a variety of contexts.

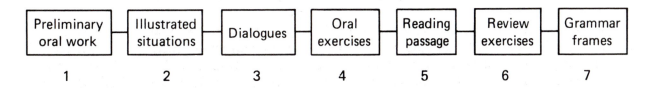

Each volume of *Practical English* is accompanied by a workbook, called *Writing Practical English.* The lessons in the workbook are closely coordinated with the lessons in the text. They provide additional writing practice in using the same grammatical structures and vocabulary.

There are also cassettes for each volume of the text—a set of four tapes per volume. The cassettes include the dialogues, stories, and pronunciation exercises in *Practical English.* They give students an opportunity to hear English spoken by native speakers representing all age groups.

The teaching methods used in this series will provide students with a good functional knowledge of grammar. Having each structure demonstrated in a variety of contexts enables students to make generalizations about the language that are reliable and useful. They develop a "language sense," a feeling for words that carries over into their daily use of English. As a result, they can say what they want to say and have it stay with them outside the classroom.

To our families—
and two very special Cariocas

ACKNOWLEDGMENTS

We wish to thank Ann Karat, Alisa Blatt, Tony Harris, Bennetta Hamilton, and Estela Cruz
for their valuable assistance in the preparation of this series.
And special thanks to Kern Krapohl for contributing some of the best stories.

Contents

CHAPTER ONE

A lot/much/many   A little/a few

a

b

a Sam Brown is a shoe repairman. He has a lot of customers, and a lot of work, so he never has much free time. Sam works hard and repairs a lot of shoes, but he doesn't make much money. That's because his prices are very low. Sam doesn't think money is very important.

1. What is Sam's job?
2. Does he have much work?
3. What about free time?
4. Does Sam make much money?
5. Are his prices high or low?
6. Does Sam think money is important?

b Johnnie Wilson is the owner of a bookshop. He has a lot of books on history and philosophy, but not many books on science or medicine. Normally, Johnnie doesn't have many customers because his books are very expensive. But today he's having a sale and there are a lot of people in his shop.

1. What kind of shop does Johnnie have?
2. Does he have many books on history and philosophy?
3. What about science and medicine?
4. Does Johnnie normally have many customers?
5. What about today?

AFFIRMATIVE

Johnnie has a lot of books.
_____ magazines.
_____ postcards.
_____ paper.

c *Make sentences with **a lot of**.*

Examples: Dr. Pasto is very popular.
He has a lot of friends.

He speaks nine languages.
He speaks a lot of languages.

1. He has a dozen dictionaries.
2. He collects hundreds of butterflies.
3. He often drinks tea.
4. Mr. Bascomb has fourteen employees.
5. He's a rich man.
6. He knows everyone in town.
7. He has a large library.
8. Anne often buys records.
9. Jimmy and Linda are very popular.

MR. BASCOMB:	My shoes look good, Sam.
SAM BROWN:	Thank you, Mr. Bascomb.

MR. BASCOMB:	How much money do I owe you?
SAM BROWN:	A dollar and fifty cents.

MR. BASCOMB:	That isn't much.
SAM BROWN:	It's a lot of money for some people.

TINO:	I saw Anne yesterday. She didn't look very well.
BARBARA:	She has a lot of problems, Tino.
TINO:	Does Anne have many friends?
BARBARA:	No, she doesn't have very many.
TINO:	Does she ever go out and have fun?
BARBARA:	No, not very often. It's a shame.

INTERROGATIVE

Does Sam have much money?   Does Anne have many friends?
_____ time?   _____ clothes?
_____ fun?   _____ hobbies?

d *Make questions with **much** or **many**.*

Examples: Sam has a lot of customers. (friends)
Does he have many friends?

He has a lot of work. (money)
Does he have much money?

1. Mrs. Golo buys a lot of bread. (milk)
2. She has a lot of glasses. (cups)
3. She drinks a lot of coffee. (tea)
4. She puts a lot of cream in her coffee. (sugar)
5. She eats a lot of fruit. (vegetables)
6. Albert eats a lot of hot dogs. (hamburgers)
7. He drinks a lot of tomato juice. (orange juice)
8. Barney meets a lot of people. (pretty girls)
9. He has a lot of free time. (fun)

NEGATIVE

Sam doesn't have much money.   Anne doesn't have many friends.
_____ time.   _____ clothes.
_____ fun.   _____ hobbies.

e *Make negative sentences with **much** or **many**.*

Examples: Johnnie has a lot of books. (customers)
But he doesn't have many customers.

Anne has a lot of free time. (fun)
But she doesn't have much fun.

1. Mr. Bascomb has a lot of money. (free time)
2. He has a lot of employees. (friends)
3. He smokes a lot of cigars. (cigarettes)
4. He drinks a lot of coffee. (tea)
5. Nancy reads a lot of magazines. (books)
6. She writes a lot of postcards. (letters)
7. She has a lot of envelopes. (paper)
8. She goes to a lot of movies. (plays)
9. Her car uses a lot of gas. (oil)

a

b

a   Jack Grubb is the owner of a popular snack bar. He's a good guy, but he's lazy. He works only a few hours a day. Jack usually has a lot of customers, but tonight there's a football game and a lot of his regular customers went to see it. There are only a few people in Jack's snack bar at the moment.

1. Who's the man behind the counter?
2. Is he the owner of a restaurant or a snack bar?
3. Does he work hard?
4. Does he usually have many customers?
5. What about tonight?
6. Where did Jack's regular customers go?

b   Barbara and Tino are having breakfast at Joe's Coffee Shop. Tino has a big appetite, and he's eating a lot this morning. He's having bacon and eggs, three slices of bread, a cup of coffee and an apple. Barbara isn't very hungry. She's only having some coffee for breakfast. She likes her coffee with a little sugar.

1. Where are Barbara and Tino having breakfast?
2. How much is Tino eating?
3. What's he having this morning?
4. Is Barbara hungry?
5. What's she having for breakfast?
6. How does she like her coffee?

COUNTABLES

Jack is talking to a few customers.

_____ *several* friends.
_____ *few* people.
_____ *some* men.

UNCOUNTABLES

She likes her coffee with a little sugar.

_____ *without much* cream.
_____ *some* milk.

a tiny bit

c   *Make sentences using* ***a little*** *and* ***a few***.

Examples: knives
There are a few knives on the shelf.

flour
There's a little flour on the shelf.

1. sugar
2. glasses
3. dishes
4. coffee
5. tea
6. bottles
7. jam
8. forks
9. spoons

knives   forks   spoons
(knife)   (fork)   (spoon)

SUSIE: You're doing a good job, Marty.

Martin
MARTY: Thanks, Susie. Can you give me a little help?

SUSIE: Sure. Do you have another brush?

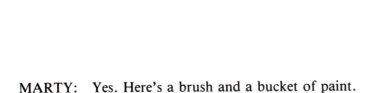

MARTY: Yes. Here's a brush and a bucket of paint.

SUSIE: Marty, there's only a little paint left in the bucket.

MARTY: Don't worry. There's more paint on the wagon.

SUSIE: What else do you have on the wagon?

MARTY: Just some old comic books.

SUSIE: Can I borrow a few of your comic books?

MARTY: Okay, but take only a few. I don't have very many.

SUSIE: Gee, these are really good. I like this story about Superman.

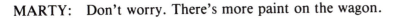

MARTY: Susie, are you going to help me or not?

SUSIE: Sure, but I can stay only a few more minutes. My mother is waiting for me.

d *Look at the pictures and make a sentence for each one, using* **a lot of,** *only a little,* **and** *only a* **few.**

1

_____ leaves on the tree.

There are <u>only a few</u> leaves on the tree.

2

_____ gas in the tank.

There's <u>only a little</u> gas in the tank.

3

Only _____ *an* orange juice in the bottle.

4

a lot of milk in the refrigerator.

5

only a few books in the bookcase.

6

Only a little mustard in the jar.

7

a lot of magazines on the desk.

8

Only a few people in the restaurant.

Mr. Bascomb is a good musician. He can play the piano and the violin. He loves classical music, and plays a lot of compositions by Mozart. Mr. Bascomb doesn't know many modern compositions, but he enjoys a lot of today's music. On Saturday afternoons he practices with a few friends. They play well together, but they don't have much time for their music. They're all busy people. At the moment, Mrs. Bascomb is serving them tea and cookies.

"Do you want a little milk with your tea, Dr. Pasto?"

"Yes please, Mrs. Bascomb."

"How many times are you going to play the same music?"

"We're going to play it a lot," says Mr. Bascomb. "Practice makes perfect."

a *Answer the following questions on the story.*

1. Is Mr. Bascomb a good musician?
2. What instruments can he play?
3. What kind of music does he like?
4. Does he know many modern compositions?
5. What does Mr. Bascomb do on Saturday afternoons?
6. Why don't Mr. Bascomb and his friends have much time for their music?
7. What's Mrs. Bascomb serving them?
8. How does Dr. Pasto like his tea?
9. Do Mr. Bascomb and his friends often play the same music?

b *Look at the picture and make sentences with **a lot of, only a few,** and **only a little.***

Examples:

milk
There's <u>a lot of</u> milk in the refrigerator.

orange juice
There's <u>only a little</u> orange juice in the refrigerator.

carrots
There are <u>only a few</u> carrots in the refrigerator.

1. ham
2. tomatoes
3. cake
4. ice cream
5. apples
6. pears
7. eggs
8. butter

c *Answer the following questions about yourself.*

1. What do you have in your refrigerator?
2. How often do you go to the market?
3. What kind of food do you like?
4. Do you eat much fruit? vegetables?
5. How many meals do you eat every day?
6. What do you usually have for breakfast? lunch? dinner?
7. What kind of desserts do you like?
8. How often do you eat out?
9. What's your favorite restaurant?

d   *Look at the pictures and make a sentence for each one using **a lot of**, **much**, and **many**.*

_____ money in the cash register.
There isn't <u>much</u> money in the cash register.

count
<u>many</u> clouds in the sky.
There aren't <u>many</u> clouds in the sky.

_____ girls at the party.

<u>a lot of</u> food on the table.

<u>a little</u> water in the bottle.

count
_____ candles on the cake.

dead give a away
_____ shoes in the closet.

not much furniture in the room.

e   *Write questions with how much and how many.*

many much. question. 문제입니다

Examples:

Peter took some photographs.   *How many photographs did he take?*

Mrs. Golo bought some flour.   *How much flour did she buy?*

1. Linda got some paper. ___How much paper did she get?___

2. She wrote some letters. ___How many letters did she write?___

3. She played some records. ___How many records did she play?___

4. She made some lemonade. ___How much lemonade did she make?___

5. Johnnie sold some books. ___How many books did Johnnies sell?___

6. He made some money. ___How much money did he make?___

7. He bought some pens. ___How many pens did he buy?___

8. He took some magazines. ___How many magazines did he take?___

9. Otis and Gloria had some free time. ___How much free time did they have___

10. They met some people. ___How many people did they meet?___

11. They drank some coffee. ___How much coffee did they drink?___

12. They ate some fruit. ___How much fruit did they eat?___

How many vegetable?

f   *Ask and answer questions as indicated.*

Example: write/letters
Student A: **Do you write many letters?**
Student B: **Yes, I write a lot of letters.**
          OR: **No, I don't write many letters.   (I write very few letters.)**

Example: have/free time
Student A: **Do you have much free time?**
Student B: **Yes, I have a lot of free time.**
          OR: **No, I don't have much free time.   (I have very little free time.)**

1. have/work	7. buy/food *much*
2. have/fun	8. eat/fruit *much*
3. see/movies	9. drink/milk
4. read/books	10. play/sports *many*
5. do/homework	11. meet/interesting people *many*
6. get/letters	12. know/artists

Home work
write question
How much?
" many?   (2 or 3)

How many times did you practice piano
How much money did you spend
when you go to grocery store?

g   *Change the following sentences using so.*

Examples: Sam never has much free time because he has a lot of work.
           Sam has a lot of work, so he never has much free time.

           He doesn't make much money because his prices are very low.
           His prices are very low, so he doesn't make much money.

1. Johnnie doesn't have many customers because his books are very expensive.
2. Anne takes the bus to work because she doesn't have a car.
3. She didn't go to work yesterday because she was sick.
4. Mr. Bascomb doesn't have much time for his music because he's a busy man.
5. He works hard because he wants to make a lot of money.
6. Linda can't go out today because she has a lot of homework.
7. We stayed home yesterday because the weather wasn't very good.
8. Barney never goes to discotheques because he doesn't like pop music.
9. Barbara is only having some coffee for breakfast because she isn't very hungry.

h   *Complete the following sentences using suitable prepositions.*

Examples: Peter is going to drive ___*to*___ the beach ___*on*___ Sunday.

1. Mr. Brown is paying ___*for*___ his daughter's education.

2. She's very popular _____ her friends _____ school.

3. Simon left ___*on*___ New York last night.

4. We thanked him ___*of*___ his help.

5. That woman is married ___*with*___ a doctor.

6. They live ___*in*___ the house across the street _____ ours.

7. Miss Jones put the table ___*out*___ the corner ___*in*___ the room.

8. She gave her pen ___*to*___ another secretary.

9. I usually write ___*on*___ a pencil.

i   *Answer the following questions about yourself.*

1. Are you enjoying your English class?
2. How do you come to class?
3. Are you living with your family?
4. What do you do in your free time?
5. How often do you see your friends?
6. What did you do last night?
7. What time did you go to bed?
8. When did you leave home this morning? Did you take the bus?
9. What are you going to do tonight? this weekend?

ONE STEP FURTHER

Mr. Bascomb often plays classical music.
1. What kind of music do you like?
2. Who's your favorite singer? musician?
3. What kind of music is popular in your country?

SKETCH

Select one student to be Johnnie Wilson. Select another student to be a customer at
   Johnnie's book store.
Situation: the customer buys a book and Johnnie gives the customer too much change.
   The customer counts the money and then tells Johnnie he made a mistake.

CONVERSATION PRACTICE

1. Pairs of students discuss their favorite singers and musicians.
2. Pairs of students discuss their favorite pastimes or hobbies.

COMPOSITION

1. Describe a famous singer, musician, or musical group. Why are they popular?
   Describe their music.
2. Write about your favorite pastime or hobby.

VOCABULARY

arrive	comic book	full (adj.)	lazy	or	science
	cream (n.)	fun	leaf	out	sell (v.)
bacon			low	owe	serve (v.)
blue	describe	group (n.)		owner	sky
bookshop	discotheque	guy	meal		snack (n.)
brush (n.)	dozen		medicine	paint (n.)	so (conj.)
bucket		hard (adv.)	musical	pastime	spoon (n.)
	else	help (n.)		philosophy	sure
carrot	everyone	hobby	normally	practice (n.)	
cash register				practice (v.)	thank (v.)
cent	few (adj.)	instrument	off (prep.)		
close (adj.)	few (pron.)		okay	repairman	wagon
cloud (n.)	fork	jam (n.)	only		what (adj.)
collect					

EXPRESSIONS

It's a shame.   Practice makes perfect.   Gee.
Go out and have fun.   a few hours a day   Thanks.

PRONUNCIATION

uw

fruit	school	movie
juice	newspaper	include
soup	stupid	shampoo
food	student	afternoon

Bruce likes fruit juice and soup.
My new shoes are blue.

e

cup	love	young
lunch	money	husband
bus	hungry	subject
truck	study	discuss

The bus stop is in front of the drugstore.
Sometimes my brother studies after lunch.

There's a blue truck in front of the school.
Do the students study in the summer?

Affirmative

| He has | a lot of | money. |
| | | friends. |

Negative

| He doesn't have | much money. |
| | many friends. |

Interrogative

| Does he have | much money? |
| | many friends? |

COUNTABLES AND UNCOUNTABLES

| They have | a lot of | sugar. |
| | | oranges. |

| They have | a little sugar. |
| | a few oranges. |

HOW MUCH/HOW MANY

| How much sugar | do they have? |
| How many oranges | |

BECAUSE/SO

She went to the market **because** there was no food in the refrigerator.
There was no food in the refrigerator, **so** she went to the market.

CHAPTER TWO

Like to/want to/ have to

Present continuous for future

Nancy likes to fly her airplane.

Otis and Gloria like to walk in the park.

Sam and Mabel want to live on a farm.

Peter wants to visit Africa.

a   *What do they like to do?*

1

Sam and Jimmy like to fish.

2

Mabel likes to cook.

3

Peter _likes to drive_

4

Barbara and Tino _like to play tennis_

5

Dr. Pasto _likes to catch some Butterflies_

6

Otis _likes to paint_

7

Mr. and Mrs. Bascomb _like to read the Newspaper_

8

Anne _likes to sing_

INTERROGATIVE   *ask question*

Does Jack like to work?   Do they like to get up early?
_____ he _____?   ___ we _____?
_____ Nancy _____?   ___ you _____?
_____ she _____?   ___ I _____?

b   *Make questions with **like to**.*

Examples: Albert doesn't like to play basketball.   (football)
            Does he like to play football?

            Linda and Jane don't like to wear dresses.   (jeans)
            Do they like to wear jeans?

1. Otis doesn't like to eat meat.   (fish)
2. He doesn't like to go to the beach.   (to the park)
3. Sam and Mabel don't like to play cards.   (chess)
4. They don't like to work in the house.   (in the garden)
5. She doesn't like to read the newspaper.   (magazines)
6. He doesn't like to talk about politics.   (sports)
7. Jimmy and Linda don't like to study at night.   (in the morning)
8. Mr. Bascomb doesn't like to smoke cigarettes.   (cigars)
9. He doesn't like to drink tea.   (coffee)

NEGATIVE

Jack doesn't like to work.   They don't like to get up early.
He _____.   We _____.
Nancy _____.   You _____.
She_____.   I _____.

c   *Answer the following questions in the negative.*

Examples: Why doesn't Barney shave more often?
            Because he doesn't like to shave.

            Why don't Sam and Mabel have parties more often?
            Because they don't like to have parties.

1. Why don't Mr. and Mrs. Golo clean the house more often?
2. Why don't they go to the market more often?
3. Why doesn't she cook dinner more often?
4. Why doesn't he wash the dishes more often?
5. Why doesn't Jack cut the grass more often?
6. Why doesn't he write more often?
7. Why doesn't he travel more often?
8. Why doesn't Anne go out more often?
9. Why doesn't she take the bus more often?

d *What do they want to do?*

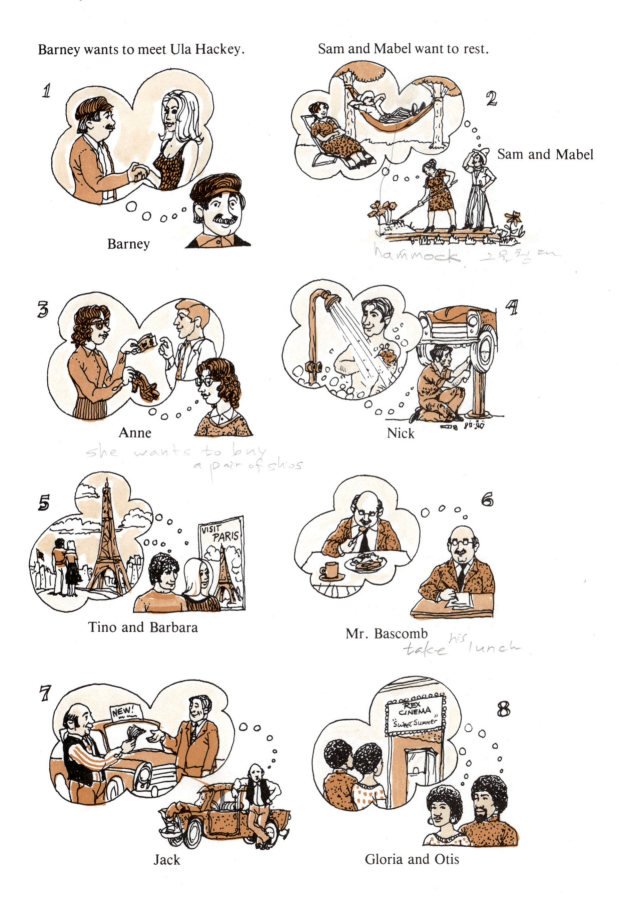

Barney wants to meet Ula Hackey.

Sam and Mabel want to rest.

1

Barney

2

Sam and Mabel

3

Anne

4

Nick

5

Tino and Barbara

6

Mr. Bascomb

7

Jack

8

Gloria and Otis

INTERROGATIVE

Does Jimmy want to study this afternoon?   Do they want to go to the library?
_____ he _____?   __ we _____?
_____ Linda _____?   __ you _____?
_____ she _____?   __ I _____?

e   *Make questions with* **want to.**

Examples: Otis and Gloria don't want to see a play.   (a movie)
           Do they want to see a movie?

           Barney doesn't want to meet Daisy Humple.   (Ula Hackey)
           Does he want to meet Ula Hackey?

1. Barbara and Tino don't want to visit Berlin.   (Paris)
2. She doesn't want to learn German.   (French)
3. Mr. and Mrs. Brown don't want to live in a big city.   (on a farm)
4. They don't want to buy a new refrigerator.   (a new stove)
5. Peter and Maria don't want to play cards.   (chess)
6. They don't want to listen to the radio.   (records)
7. Nancy doesn't want to dance with Fred.   (Barney)
8. She doesn't want to talk about sports.   (music)
9. Jack doesn't want to buy a motorcycle.   (a new car)

NEGATIVE

Jimmy doesn't want to study this afternoon.   They don't want to go to the library.
He _____.   We _____.
Linda _____.   You _____.
She _____.   I _____.

f   *Answer the following questions in the negative.*

Examples: Why doesn't Peter sell his car?
           He doesn't want to sell his car.

           Why don't Sam and Mabel paint their house?
           They don't want to paint their house.

1. Why don't Sam and Mabel buy a new refrigerator?
2. Why doesn't Linda call her boyfriend?
3. Why doesn't she go out tonight?   *She got into a fight with her boyfriend*
4. Why doesn't Nancy get married?
5. Why doesn't she live with her family?   *She wants to be free*
6. Why don't Mr. and Mrs. Golo sell their house?
7. Why don't they get an apartment?
8. Why doesn't Barbara leave her job?
9. Why doesn't she find another job?

a   It's a beautiful summer day. Tino wants to go to the park and play tennis. But he can't leave the restaurant. He has to stay and help his father. There are a lot of customers today, and Tino has to take their orders.

1. What kind of day is it?
2. What does Tino want to do?
3. Why can't he go to the park?
4. Who does he have to help?
5. Are there many customers today?
6. Does Tino have to take their orders?

He's stuck at work

b   There's a good movie playing at the Rex Cinema today. It's a western with Tex Laredo called *The Last Texan*. Linda wants to go and see it. But first she has to clean the kitchen and wash the dishes. Then she can go to the movies.

1. What movie is playing at the Rex Cinema?
2. Who's in it?
3. What does Linda want to do?
4. What does she have to do first?
5. What does Jimmy have to do today?

AFFIRMATIVE

must

Tino has to work today.
He _____.
Linda _____.
She _____.

They have to wash the dishes.
We _____.
You _____.
I _____.

c   *Make sentences with* **has to** *or* **have to**.

Examples: Tino can't play tennis this afternoon.   (stay at the restaurant)
He has to stay at the restaurant.

Sam and Mabel can't sleep late.   (get up at six o'clock)
They have to get up at six o'clock.

1. Mrs. Golo can't watch television.   (make dinner)
2. Jimmy and Linda can't go to the party tonight.   (study)
3. Barney can't play cards with Nancy.   (cut the grass)
4. The students can't talk in class.   (be quiet)
5. Jack can't go to the football game tonight.   (work)
6. Anne can't go to lunch now.   (type some letters)
7. Mr. and Mrs. Bascomb can't eat dessert.   (lose weight)
8. Maria can't talk on the telephone.   (wash the dishes)
9. Peter can't go home.   (stay at the office)

MR. BASCOMB:	What are you looking at?
MRS. BASCOMB:	The sky. It's getting cloudy.
MR. BASCOMB:	Do you think it's going to rain?
MRS. BASCOMB:	I hope not. I have to go to the store.
MR. BASCOMB:	Can't you go tomorrow?
MRS. BASCOMB:	No, I have to go now. I have to get some food for dinner.
MR. BASCOMB:	Don't worry about dinner. We can go to a restaurant tonight.

OTIS:	Can you go out today, Gloria?
GLORIA:	I don't think so, Otis. I have to paint this room.
OTIS:	Do you have to do it now?
GLORIA:	I'm afraid so. I'm expecting some guests this weekend.
OTIS:	I can help you. I'm pretty good with a brush.
GLORIA:	That's nice of you. We can go out afterwards.

d   *Answer the following questions about the pictures, as indicated.*

1. A: **Does Mrs. Bascomb have to make dinner tonight?**
   B: **No, she doesn't.**
   A: **Why not?**
   B: **Because she's going to a restaurant.**

2. A: **Do Anne and Barbara have to be nice to Mr. Bascomb?**
   B: **Yes, they do.**
   A: **Why?**
   B: **Because he's the boss.**

3. Does Dr. Pasto have to water the plants today?

4. Does Maria have to go to the market?

5. Do Jimmy and Linda have to be quiet?

6. Does Peter have to get some gas soon?

the needle is on full

7. Do these men have to hurry?

Because they just robbed a grocery store

8. Do these men have to pay for their food?

they are in jail. prison

JOHNNIE: Hi, Maria. What are you doing
           tonight?

MARIA: I'm seeing a movie with Peter.

JOHNNIE: Are you meeting him at the theater?

MARIA: No, we're going in his car.

JOHNNIE: What are you doing after the movie?

MARIA: We're having dinner at a Mexican
           restaurant.

JOHNNIE: Well, have a good time.

MARIA: Thanks, Johnnie. See you later.

PRESENT CONTINUOUS for the FUTURE

They're meeting their friends tonight.
_____ attending a lecture _____.
_____ going to the movies _____.
_____ eating out _____.

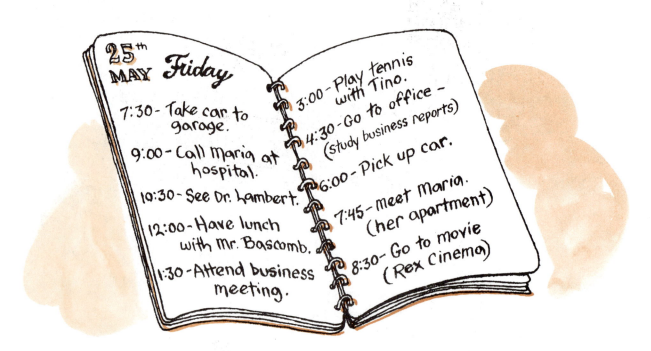

e *Look at Peter's schedule for Friday. Ask and answer questions about what he's doing at different hours of the day.*

    Example: 7:30—Take car to garage
           Student A: **What's he doing at seven-thirty?**
           Student B: **He's taking his car to the garage.**

f *Answer the following questions about yourself, using the present continuous.*

    Example: What are you doing after class?
           I'm meeting a friend.   **(going to the library, etc.)**

1. What are you doing tonight?
2. Are you eating out tonight?
3. What are you doing tomorrow morning?
4. Are you getting up early tomorrow?
5. What are you doing tomorrow afternoon?
6. Are you going out tomorrow night?
7. Are you going out Friday night?
8. What are you doing this Saturday?
9. Are you going to a movie this weekend?

Mr. Bascomb likes to save money so he usually walks to work. Last Friday, however, he was late, so he called a cab. A few minutes later, a taxi pulled up in front of his house. Mr. Bascomb kissed his wife goodbye and got in the taxi. The driver was Barney Field.

"Hello," he said. "Aren't you Mr. Bascomb, president of City Bank?"

"That's right," said Mr. Bascomb.

"How did you know?"

"That was easy," replied Barney.

"I read it on your briefcase. Besides, I went to your bank every day last week. I want to borrow some money."

"Oh really," said Mr. Bascomb. "What do you want the money for?"

"I want to fix up my cab," said Barney. "It doesn't run very well. The engine makes a lot of noise and I'm losing customers because of it. I also have to get some new tires."

"That's true," said Mr. Bascomb. "I can see you have a problem." "

On the way to the bank, Mr. Bascomb talked to Barney. He liked Barney's friendly personality and careful driving. When the cab pulled up in front of the bank, Mr. Bascomb got out and said to the driver,

"Barney, I like you. I'm going to give you the money. How much do you need for repairs?"

"About $400."

"OK," said Mr. Bascomb, "come and see me at the bank on Monday."

Barney was very happy. "Thank you very much, Mr. Bascomb," he said. "There's just one thing."

"Yes, Barney, what is it?"

"You owe me $1.25 for taxi fare."

"But Barney," said Mr. Bascomb, "I'm going to loan you $400, and you're worried about $1.25."

Barney smiled. "I know, Mr. Bascomb, but do you want to loan your money to a bad businessman?"

a   *Answer the following questions about the story.*

1. Why does Mr. Bascomb usually walk to work?
2. Why did he call a cab last Friday? *He was running late.*
3. Who was the driver?
4. How did Barney know that Mr. Bascomb was president of City Bank?
5. Why does Barney want to borrow money from the bank?
6. What's wrong with Barney's cab?
7. How much does Barney need for repairs?
8. What does Mr. Bascomb like about Barney?
9. Is he going to give Barney the money?
10. Do you think Barney is a good businessman? Why?

sorry I don't want to but I have to

b   *Answer the following questions using one of these expressions: **I think so, I hope so, I'm afraid so, I don't think so, I hope not, I'm afraid not.***

Example: Is it going to rain?   **I think so.   (I'm afraid so, etc.)**
                                         I don't think so.   (I hope not, etc.)

1. Are you going to travel this year?
2. Are you going to study another language?
3. Are you going to see a movie this weekend?
4. Is this class going to end soon?
5. Are you going to see your friends after class?

6. Are you going to study tonight?
7. Does Mr. Bascomb love his wife?
8. Is he a good husband?
9. Is Barney a good businessman?

c   *How much do these things cost?*

Example: an ice cream cone
Student A: **How much is an ice cream cone?**
Student B: **About seventy-five cents.** *a dollars*

1. a pencil
2. a notebook
3. a newspaper
4. a phone call
5. an umbrella
6. a postcard

7. an apple
8. a loaf of bread
9. a coke
10. a cup of coffee
11. a toothbrush
12. a comb

 ice cream cone

 loaf of bread

 comb

d   *Ask and answer questions about the pictures, as indicated.*

1. A: **Does Barney like to shave?**
   B: **No, he doesn't.**
   A: **Why not?**
   B: **Because it hurts.**

2. A: **Do Otis and Gloria like to dance?**
   B: **Yes, they do.**
   A: **Why?**
   B: **Because it's fun.**

3. Does Anne like to talk with Dr. Pasto?

4. Does Johnnie like to ride the bus?

5. Do people like to eat at Joe's?

6. Do people like to eat at Mom's?

7. Does Otis like to paint flowers?

8. Do these men like to work?

e *Complete the following sentences with a possessive adjective or a possessive pronoun.*

Example: They painted ___*their*___ kitchen yellow. We painted ___*ours*___ white.

1. Barbara likes _____ coffee with a little sugar in it.

2. You look different. Did you cut _____ hair?

3. I'm wearing _____ favorite tie.

4. Give me that pencil. It's _____.

5. They're doing _____ homework.

6. We're going to show them _____ new apartment.

7. Those magazines belong to Mrs. Golo. They're _____.

8. Peter has a problem. He left _____ car keys at the office.

9. You can't take those envelopes because they aren't _____.

10. They're fixing up _____ apartment and we're fixing up _____.

f *Answer the following questions as indicated.*

Examples: When did Dr. Pasto live in Tokyo?   (Hong Kong)
   He didn't live in Tokyo. He lived in Hong Kong.

   Why did Gloria sell her table? (her desk)
   She didn't sell her table. She sold her desk.

1. When did Nancy go to the bank?   (to the post office)
2. When did Jimmy clean the kitchen?   (the living room)
3. When did Linda buy a raincoat?   (an umbrella)
4. Why did Sam get up at seven o'clock?   (at eight o'clock)
5. Why did Barney take the radio?   (the record player)
6. How did Fred lose his coat?   (his hat)
7. Why did Maria wear a black dress?   (a blue dress)
8. When did Peter call Barbara?   (Maria)
9. Why did Albert take a taxi?   (a bus)

g *Answer the following questions about yourself.*

1. What kind of work do you have to do at home?
2. What do you like to do with your free time?
3. Where do you want to go this weekend?
4. What sports do you like to play?
5. What are some things you have to do but don't like to do?
6. What time do you have to get up in the morning?
7. How often do you go to meetings?
8. Do you ever take a taxi?
9. How much is the bus fare in your city?

ONE STEP FURTHER

Mr. Bascomb is the president of City Bank. Barney wants to borrow money from the bank.
1. What does Barney want to do with the money?
2. What are some reasons people borrow money from the bank?
3. Is it easy or difficult to get a loan from the bank?
4. Do you ever borrow or loan money? What about your personal possessions?

Mr. Bascomb usually walks to work because he likes to save money.
1. What are some other ways that people save money?
2. How do you save money?
3. Do you try to buy food and clothes when they are on sale?

SKETCH

Select one student to be a banker. Select another student to be an applicant for a loan.
Situation: the loan applicant wants to borrow money from the bank. The banker is sympa-
  thetic but wants to know all the facts, for example, what the money is for, where the
  applicant will get or earn the money to pay back the loan, etc.

COMPOSITION

Be original   be creative.

1. What are some of the things you like to do? Why do you enjoy these activities?
2. What are some of the things you want to do? What's the difference between what you are
   doing now and what you want to do?
3. What are some of the things you have to do? Contrast the things you want or like to do
   with the things you have to do.

VOCABULARY

afterwards	cook (v.)	fare (n.)	lecture (n.)	pick (v.)	save (v.)
although	cost (v.)	farm (n.)	loan (n.)	possession	sleep (v.)
		fish (v.)	loan (v.)		so (adv.)
besides	driving (n.)	fix (v.)		rain (v.)	
briefcase		fly (v.)	noise	repair (n.)	Texan
	engine			reply (v.)	tire (n.)
cab	expect	hope (v.)	order (n.)	right (adj.)	try (v.)
cinema		however		run (v.)	

EXPRESSIONS

on the way   That's nice of you.

PRONUNCIATION

p

pan	airplane	happy
peach	hospital	trip
pack	important	sleep
pen	repair	envelope

The Japanese airplane disappeared over Pakistan.
The passengers planned a party for the pilot.
He painted pretty pictures in the park.

b

bad	about	table
beach	nobody	club
back	number	job
Ben	husband	cab

Barney belongs to the Bombay Bicycle Club.
He borrows books from the nearby library.
Nobody knows about the busy cab driver.

Mr. Baker has an important job at the post office.
Perhaps Mabel is at the bus stop.
Albert put the cup by the teapot.

LIKE TO / WANT TO / HAVE TO
Affirmative

He She	likes to wants to has to	get up early. make breakfast. go to the market.
I You We They	like to want to have to	

Negative

He She	doesn't (does not)	like to want to have to	get up early. make breakfast. go to the market.
I You We They	don't (do not)		

Interrogative

Does	he she	like to want to have to	get up early? make breakfast? go to the market?
Do	I you we they		

Short Answers

Yes,	he she	does.
	I you we they	do.

No,	he she	doesn't.
	I you we they	don't.

Is it going to rain?

I think so. I hope so. I'm afraid so.

I don't think so. I hope not. I'm afraid not.

PRESENT CONTINUOUS FOR FUTURE
Affirmative

They're	arriving on Monday. staying at the Wickam Hotel. leaving on Thursday.

Negative

They aren't	arriving on Monday. staying at the Wickam Hotel. leaving on Thursday.

Interrogative

Are they	arriving on Monday? staying at the Wickam Hotel? leaving on Thursday?

Short Answers

Yes, they are.

No, they aren't.

CHAPTER THREE

Both/neither/all/none
"Which (one) . . . ?"

Some/any compounds
Must (logical conclusion)

Both of these men are strong.
Neither of them is weak.

Both of these women are young.
Neither of them is old.

All of these bottles are empty.
None of them are full.

All of these watches are expensive.
None of them are cheap.

a   *Look at the pictures and make two sentences for each one, using **all**, **none**, **both**, and **neither**.*

1

2

men / sick / well
All of these men are sick.
None of them are well.

girls / sad / happy
Neither of these girls is sad.
Both of them are happy.

3

4

boys / fat / thin

women / tall / short

5

6

glasses / full / empty

cameras / cheap / expensive

Neither is cheap.

7

8

shoes / clean / dirty

guns / old / new

All of these shoes are dirty.
None of them are clean

pistols

Both of these guns is old.
Neither is new.

9

10

men / rich / poor

women / beautiful / ugly

ALBERT: Hello, Mrs. Brown. Where's Linda?

MRS. BROWN: She went to the museum.

ALBERT: Which one did she go to?

MRS. BROWN: She went to the Art Museum.

ALBERT: Did she walk?

MRS. BROWN: No, she took the bus.

ALBERT: Which bus did she take?

MRS. BROWN: The red one, number thirty-six.

SAM BROWN: Can you show me the hat on the shelf?

SALESMAN: Which hat, the brown one or the gray one?

SAM BROWN: The brown one.

SALESMAN: Here, try it on. Let's see how it looks.

SAM BROWN: Hmm. It's not exactly the right size.

SALESMAN: Let's try the other one.

b   *Ask and answer questions about the pictures. Use appropriate adjectives.*

1. Men's Hats

CUSTOMER: Can you show me the <u>hat</u>, please?

SALESPERSON: Which <u>hat</u>, the <u>brown</u> one or the <u>gray</u> one?

CUSTOMER: The <u>brown</u> one.

2. Dresses

3. Handbags *large & small*

4. umbrellas

5. watches

$250 $30

6. Dolls

7. ☆CARS☆

NEW   USED

PETER: Hello, Sandy. Are you waiting for someone?

SANDY: No, I'm not waiting for anyone.

PETER: Good. Let's go somewhere.

SANDY: Where do you want to go?

PETER: Anywhere. How about the zoo?

SANDY: That sounds like fun. Let's go.

ANNE: There's something here for you, Barbara.

BARBARA: What is it? Anything important?

ANNE: It's a box of chocolates from Tino.

BARBARA: Oh, he's always sending me something.

ANNE: You're lucky. I never get anything.

BARBARA: That's too bad. Here, have a chocolate.

AFFIRMATIVE   NEGATIVE

She's waiting for someone.   She isn't waiting for anyone.
_____ reading something.   _____ reading anything.
_____ going somewhere.   _____ going anywhere.

a *Answer the following questions as indicated.*

Example: Barbara is writing to someone, isn't she?
          No, she isn't writing to anyone.

1. Anne is going somewhere next week, isn't she?
2. She knows someone in New York, doesn't she?
3. She's going to buy something, isn't she?
4. Barney is driving somewhere, isn't he?
5. He's going to meet someone, isn't he?
6. He's worried about something, isn't he?
7. Nancy is expecting someone, isn't she?
8. She's planning something, isn't she?
9. She's going somewhere with Barney, isn't she?

INTERROGATIVE

Is she waiting for anyone?
_____ reading anything?
_____ going anywhere?

b *Make questions with **anyone, anything,** and **anywhere**.*

Examples: Barbara got a box of chocolates. (Anne)
           Did Anne get anything?

           Peter and Sandy went to the zoo. (Albert and Linda)
           Did Albert and Linda go anywhere?

           They saw their friends at the park. (you)
           Did you see anyone at the park?

1. Maria lost her handbag at the party. (Gloria) *Did Gloria lose anything?*
2. Barbara danced with Tino. (Anne)
3. Mr. Bascomb went to the movies. (his wife)
4. They bought a table yesterday. (Dr. Pasto)
5. Mabel wrote to her mother. (Sam)
6. Mrs. Golo had coffee and eggs for breakfast. (Mr. Golo)
7. Barney went to the park. (Fred)
8. They called Mr. Bascomb. (you)
9. Nick stopped at the drugstore after work. (you)

MABEL: Where's your friend Jack? I hardly ever see him.

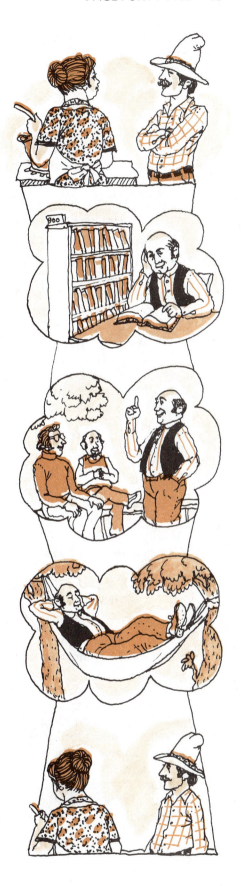

SAM: He's always at the library.

MABEL: He must read a lot.

SAM: He does. And he can discuss anything.

MABEL: He must be intelligent.

SAM: He is. But he doesn't like to work.

MABEL: He must be lazy, too.

Jack can discuss anything.
Nancy_____.
They   _____.
You_____.

He must be intelligent.
She   _____.
They_____.
You   _____.

c   *Make sentences with **must be** + adjective.*

Examples: Sam worked very hard today.
            He must be tired.

            Tino can lift anything.
            He must be strong.

1. Jack doesn't like to work.
2. Barney found a ten-dollar bill.
3. Maria lost her handbag. *She must be furious*
4. Everyone likes Dr. Pasto. *He must be popular.*
5. Anne takes three showers a day.
6. Mr. Bascomb didn't go to work today.
7. Albert is having three hamburgers for lunch.
8. He wants five glasses of milk.
9. Ula Hackey has a big house, two cars, and a lot of expensive clothes.

They're always at school.
_____ at the office.
_____ in the kitchen.
_____ on the telephone.

They must study a lot.
_____ work ____.
_____ cook ____.
_____ talk ____.

d   *Make sentences with **must** + verb + **a lot**.*

Examples: Fred is always in bed.
            He must sleep a lot.

            Otis and Gloria often go to the
            discotheque.
            They must dance a lot.

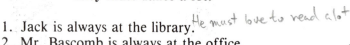

1. Jack is always at the library. *He must love to read a lot*
2. Mr. Bascomb is always at the office.
3. Barbara is a good tennis player.
4. Nancy is a good pilot.
5. Peter knows Europe very well.
6. Albert is very fat.
7. Mrs. Brown is always in the kitchen.
8. Linda is always on the telephone. *she must run up a huge bill.*
9. The children are always in the park.

Peter is at the bookshop. He wants to get Maria a book for her birthday.
The other day Nancy recommended a book called *The Voyage of the Cat*.
But Peter was in a hurry, and now he can't remember anything she told
him. One of the salesgirls is trying to help Peter.

"Was it some kind of historical book?" she asks.

"No, it wasn't anything historical," he says. "It was a new book
by someone with a funny name."

"Well," she says, "all the new books are on this shelf. Is it one of
these?"

"No, it's none of those. But now I remember. The author's name
is Ken Killuga."

"Of course," says the salesgirl. "We have two books by Ken
Killuga in the window. Which one do you want?"

"I still can't remember."

"Why don't you take both of them?"

"I can't," says Peter. "They're very expensive, and perhaps neither
of them is the one she wants."

"Whatever you say," says the salesgirl.
She smiles at Peter. "I think your girlfriend
is very lucky. She must be intelligent, too."

"You're right, she is. But how did
you know?"

"It's obvious. She has such a pleasant,
good-looking boyfriend."

"Well, thank you," says Peter, smiling
happily. "On second thought, I'll take
both books."

a *Answer the following questions about the story.*

1. Where's Peter?
2. Who does he want to get a book for?
3. What's the name of the book that Nancy recommended?
4. Why can't Peter remember the title?
5. Who's trying to help Peter?
6. What's the name of the author?
7. How many of Ken Killuga's books are in the window?
8. Why doesn't Peter take both of them right away?
9. Why does the salesgirl think Peter's girlfriend is lucky?
10. Why does Peter decide to take both books?

b *Make questions with **who, what,** or **where.***

Examples: Peter went somewhere.
  Where did he go?

  He talked to someone.
  Who did he talk to?

  He bought something.
  What did he buy?

1. Anne went somewhere last night.
2. She saw someone in the park. *Who did she see?*
3. He had something in his briefcase. *What did he have?*
4. Otis met someone at the party. *Who did she meet?*
5. He gave her something. *What did he give to her?*
6. They went somewhere after the party. *Where did they go*
7. Barney found something yesterday. *Who did find / sawith y. When did Barney find something*
8. He showed it to someone. *Who did he show it to?*
9. They left it somewhere. *Where did they leave it*

c *Complete the following sentences.*

Example: Linda went to the Art Museum *to look at the paintings.*

1. Mrs. Golo stopped at the drug store *to buy aspirin* _____

2. Did your sister go downtown _____

3. I'm going to the department store *to shop (for)* _____

4. My friends are going home _____

5. Mr. Bascomb is stopping at the post office _____

6. Did the boys go to the park _____

7. We went to the zoo _____

8. Jack is going to the library _____

9. Are you stopping at the market _____

After Peter left the bookstore, he ran into Tino on the street. Tino noticed the package under Peter's arm.

TINO: What do you have there, Peter?

PETER: Some books. I got them for Maria.

TINO: Were they expensive?

PETER: Yes. I paid forty dollars for them.

TINO: Where did you get them?

PETER: At Johnnie's Bookstore.

d *Ask and answer questions about the pictures, as in the conversation above.*

A: What do you have there, _____?

B: _____. I got it/them for
     _____.

A: _____ expensive?

B: Yes. I paid _____ for it/them.

     OR   No. I only paid _____ for
          it/them. *not really*

A: Where did you get _____?

B: At _____.

e *Make sentences using **both, neither, all,** and **none.***

Examples: Both of those women are intelligent.
            Neither of them is stupid.

            None of these books are cheap.
            All of them are expensive.

1. Both of those boys are tall.
2. All of those men are sick.
3. None of them are happy.
4. Neither of these hats is good-looking.
5. Both of them are cheap.

6. All of those oranges are good.
7. None of these bottles are full.
8. Neither of these glasses are clean.
9. Both of them are small.

f *Write short sentences showing that you disagree with the following statements.*

Examples: Peter didn't go to the bookstore yesterday. *Yes, he did.*

He was at the office all day. *No, he wasn't.*

1. Fred is lazy. _*no, he isn't*_

2. He never does any work. _*Yes, he does*_

3. He didn't buy those flowers. _*Yes, he did*_

4. His sister bought them. _*No, she didn't*_

5. The flowers were expensive. _*No, they weren't*_

6. We have to go now. _*No, we don't*_

7. We don't have much time. _*Yes, we do*_

8. We're going to be late. _*No, we arn't*_

9. Your friends can't help us. _*Yes, they can*_

10. They're too busy. _*No, they aua't*_

g *Complete the following sentences using **some, any,** or **one.***

Examples: Linda needs some envelopes. She doesn't have _*any*_ .

Jimmy doesn't have any toothpaste. He needs _*some*_ .

I need a dictionary. I don't have _*one*_ .

1. Anne has a typewriter at work, but she doesn't have _____ at home.

2. There isn't any food in the refrigerator. We have to buy _____.

3. Tino needs some shampoo. He doesn't have _____.

4. Barbara bought two hats. _____ is white and the other is yellow.

5. I need some money and hope to borrow _____ from Mr. Bascomb.

6. Nancy got some interesting letters last week. _____ of them was from Rome.

7. She's going to buy some new dishes although she doesn't need _____.

8. Linda made some cookies yesterday and Mabel made _____ last week.

9. Give those cookies to Albert. I don't want _____.

10. He has a camera, but it's not a very good _____.

h   *The people in these pictures are talking with their hands. Can you tell what they are saying? Write an appropriate sentence for each one. There can be more than one appropriate sentence for each picture.*

Do these gestures mean the same thing all over the world? What are some other things you can say with your hands?

i   *Answer the following questions about yourself.*

1. Do all of your friends like music?
2. Do any of your friends play the guitar?
3. Are you thinking about any of your friends now?
4. Are you going to meet anyone after class?
5. Are you going anywhere tonight?
6. Do you like both classical and pop music? Which do you prefer?
7. Do you like both police movies and westerns? Which do you prefer?
8. Do you have anything in your pockets?
9. Are both of your socks the same color?

ONE STEP FURTHER

The salesgirl gave Peter some nice compliments. In other words, she flattered him.
1. When and why do people use flattery?
2. Do you think flattery is OK? Why or why not?
3. What are some compliments that you give your friends?
4. What are some compliments that you get from other people?
5. Give a compliment to the person sitting next to you.

Peter likes to shop, but he doesn't have much time for it. He's a busy man.
1. Do you like to shop? Why or why not?
2. Is the service good in most stores? What is your idea of good service?
3. Can you return the merchandise if it isn't what you want?
4. Is the customer always right in your country?
5. Where do you like to shop? Why?

SKETCH

Select one student to be a salesperson. Select another student to be a customer.
Situation: the salesperson decides to use flattery on a difficult customer.

COMPOSITION

1. Write about shopping in your country. (How is it different from shopping in the U.S.A.?)
2. Write about your favorite place in the city. Where is it? When was the first time you went there? Why do you like it so much?
3. Write about your best friend. What is he/she like? What does he/she do? Why is this person special?

VOCABULARY

all (pron.)	exactly	most (adj.)	plan (v.)	shopping (n.)	voyage (n.)
anything		must (v.)	pleasant	size (n.)	
anywhere	good-looking		prefer	sociable	weak
author (n.)	gray	neither (pron.)		someone	whatever
		none (pron.)	recommend	something	which (adj.)
both (pron.)	hardly		remember	somewhere	
	historical	obvious		sound (v.)	
child		one (pron.)	salesgirl	still (adv.)	
chocolate (n.)	lift (v.)		salesman		
		perhaps	send	thought (n.)	
decide					

EXPRESSIONS

Let's see.	Whatever you say.	hardly ever	on second thought
Try it on.	That sounds like fun.	in a hurry	Hmm . . .
		of course	Well . . .

PRONUNCIATION

š

shop	ocean	wash
shame	musician	dish
shower	tradition	brush
sociable	expression	English

The short man shined his shoes.
She washed the dishes and took a shower.
Traditional Englishmen often fish in the ocean.

tš

chair	kitchen	beach
church	teacher	watch
cheap	picture	French
chocolate	question	sandwich

There's a chicken sandwich in the kitchen.
The teacher answered the children's questions.
Charlie Chan has a picture of a Chinese statue.

Miss Shipley played chess with a sociable Frenchman.
She took his cheap Spanish watch.
He chased her across the ocean to China.

ALL/NONE

All None	of those men are intelligent.

ALL

They're all intelligent.

BOTH/NEITHER

Both Neither	of these books	are is	expensive.

BOTH

They're both expensive.

Question with WHICH

He's going to the library.

Which	library one	is he going to?

Compounds of SOME and ANY

	talking to	someone.
They're	buying	something.
	going	somewhere.

Questions with WHO, WHAT, and WHERE

Who		talking to?
What	are they	buying?
Where		going?

Interrogative

	talking to	anyone?
Are they	buying	anything?
	going	anywhere?

Negative

	talking to	anyone.
They aren't	buying	anything.
	going	anywhere.

MUST

He	has a nice girlfriend. can discuss anything.

He	must be	happy. intelligent.

They	play tennis every day. often go to the library.

They	must	like tennis. read a lot.

CHAPTER FOUR

Review

Johnnie Wilson is very unhappy these days. He shares a small apartment with his Uncle Ed, and Ed is a very difficult person to live with. He has a lot of bad habits. Ed doesn't like to take a bath or change his clothes, and he never cleans up the apartment. He leaves his dirty dishes in the sink and his empty coke cans in the living room, and he never washes his dog Brutus.

When Johnnie comes home, he can't relax because Ed is always watching TV and playing his bongos. He can't sit in his favorite chair because Brutus is always there. And Johnnie can hardly breathe because of Ed's cigar smoke, which is killing Johnnie's plants.

Johnnie has to pay the rent because Ed never has any money—he's always broke. Ed is unemployed, and he says he can't find a job. But the truth is, he doesn't want to work. Ed has an easy, comfortable life, and that's the way he likes it.

Of course, Johnnie doesn't like the situation. But what can he do about it? Whenever he complains, Ed either ignores him or leaves the room. And Johnnie hates to be alone in the same room with Brutus. He knows Brutus has sharp teeth and a bad attitude.

At the moment, Johnnie is looking for some food in the refrigerator. He's very hungry after working hard all day. Unfortunately, Ed and Brutus got there first.

"You two are really disgusting!" cries Johnnie. "You took all the food and didn't leave anything for me."

"Don't worry," says Ed, his mouth full of spaghetti. "The market's still open. You can go there and buy more."

"No more!" says Johnnie, angrily. "I'm not buying any more food for you and that animal. From now on, you can pay for your own food—and the rent. I'm moving out!"

"You can't do that," says Ed, wiping his fingers on his T-shirt.

"Oh, no?" says Johnnie. "Watch me."

Ed and Brutus look very surprised as Johnnie goes to his room, packs his suitcase, and walks out of the apartment.

a   *Answer the following questions about the story.*

1. Who does Johnnie live with? *blob*
2. What are some of Ed's bad habits?
3. Why can't Johnnie relax when he comes home? *Because makes too much noise.*
4. Why can't he sit in his favorite chair? *Because Brutus is always there.*
5. Why are Johnnie's plants dying? *Because Ed's cigar smoke is killing them.*
6. Why does Johnnie have to pay the rent? *Ed is total slacker who doesn't want to work.*
7. Why doesn't Ed work?
8. What happens when Johnnie complains to Ed? *Nothing*
9. Why is Johnnie afraid of Brutus?
10. What's Johnnie doing in the kitchen?
11. Why is the refrigerator empty? *They got there first.*
12. What does Johnnie decide to do about the situation? *It's about time. finally? He finally moves out.*

b   *Answer the following questions about yourself.*

1. Do you have a roommate? Describe him/her.
2. Are you an easy person to live with?
3. Do you have any bad habits?
4. What are your good points?
5. Do you know anyone like Ed?
6. What are your neighbors like?
7. Do you ever have problems with your neighbors?
8. Do you ever complain? What things make you angry?

Johnnie sees an advertisement for a one-bedroom apartment in the newspaper. He goes to a public telephone and calls the manager.

JOHNNIE: Hello, can I speak to Miss Blake, please?

BLOSSOM: This is Blossom Blake.

JOHNNIE: Are you the manager of the Sherwood Oaks Apartments?

BLOSSOM: That's right. What can I do for you?

JOHNNIE: I'm calling about the apartment you have for rent.
Is it still available?

BLOSSOM: Yes, it is. Why don't you come and take a look at it?

JOHNNIE: OK, but I want to ask you some questions first.

BLOSSOM: Sure, what do you want to know?

JOHNNIE: Your ad says the rent is four hundred dollars a month.
Does that include utilities?

BLOSSOM: The water is included. But you pay for gas and electricity.

JOHNNIE: Is the apartment furnished?

BLOSSOM: Yes. There's a bed, sofa, dining table and two chairs.

JOHNNIE: I see. Can you tell me anything about the tenants?
What are they like?

BLOSSOM: Oh, all the tenants are nice, friendly people.

JOHNNIE: That's good. Does the apartment have a view?

BLOSSOM: Yes. There's an interesting view from the bedroom window.

JOHNNIE: Great. When can I see the apartment?

BLOSSOM: I'm here all day. Come any time you like.

JOHNNIE: I'm coming now.

BLOSSOM: Wait a minute. What's your name?

JOHNNIE: Johnnie Wilson.

BLOSSOM: See you soon, Johnnie. Bye, bye.

c   *Answer the following questions about the dialogue.*

1. Who is Blossom Blake?
2. Why is Johnnie calling her? *He is answering an ad for apartment.*
3. How did he find out about the apartment?
4. How much is the rent?
5. Are the utilities included?
6. What kind of furniture does the apartment have?
7. What are the tenants like?
8. When is Johnnie going to see the apartment? *He is going right away = now*
9. What's the address of the Sherwood Oaks Apartments?

Nebraska

***************************** **CLASSIFIED ADS** *************************

1	WICKAM CITY $335 Single unfurn. New paint, utils. incl., pool, prkg. Xlnt loc. Call Manager 264-3528	WICKAM CITY $575 Attractive 2 Bdrm. Small, clean, quiet bldg. No pets. 573-2285 after 5 pm	4
2	WICKAM CITY $425 Nice 1 Bdrm. stv/frig, A/C, balc. great view! Children OK! Call 483-2186	WICKAM CITY $600 2 bdrm., 2 ba. Utils. free, new carpet, stv/frig. Near shops & transp. 260-5097	5
3	WICKAM CITY $450 1 Bdrm. furn. laundry, prkg. Good neighborhood. Close to shopping & transp. 626-3751	WICKAM CITY $1,000 3 Bdrm. hse. Large rooms, fireplace, view, grdn. 2-car garage 574-2536 9-5 pm	6

ABBREVIATIONS

A/C	= air conditioning	cpt.	= carpet	prkg.	= parking
apt.	= apartment	frig.	= refrigerator	stv.	= stove
ba.	= bathroom	furn.	= furnished	transp.	= transportation
balc.	= balcony	grdn.	= garden	unfurn.	= unfurnished
bdrm.	= bedroom	hse.	= house	utils. incl.	= utilities included
bldg.	= building	lndry.	= laundry	xlnt. loc.	= excellent location

d   *Study the abbreviated words and then describe the apartments in the classified ads.*

Example 1: It's a single, unfurnished apartment. It has new paint and the utilities are
           included . . .

e   *Have a conversation like the one on page 58. One person is looking for an apartment and the
    other person is the manager. You can refer to the classified ads above or use your imagination.*

Student A: Phone the manager and
(1) ask him/her to describe the apartment
(2) ask for any more information you need:
    utilities? parking? other tenants? quiet?
(3) decide to go and see the apartment
(4) ask how to get there

Student B: Answer the phone and
(1) describe the apartment
(2) answer any more questions about the
    apartment (say good things about it)
(3) ask if he/she is coming to see it
(4) tell him/her how to get there

Five minutes after his telephone conversation with Miss Blake, Johnnie arrives at the Sherwood Oaks Apartments. He goes up to the manager's apartment and knocks on the door.

"I'm coming," yells Miss Blake from inside. The door opens and Blossom Blake appears. She is a thin, middle-aged woman with straight brown hair. "You must be Johnnie Wilson."

Johnnie nods his head affirmatively.

"You sure got here fast," says Blossom.

"I have to find an apartment right away," says Johnnie. "I don't have any place to stay."

"Well, this is your lucky day," says Blossom. "I have the perfect apartment for you. Come with me."

Johnnie follows Blossom down the long hallway that leads to the back of the building. He sees three men at the end of the hallway. They're sitting in a circle playing cards. Blossom frowns.

"I thought I told you boys not to play in the building."

"Sorry, Blossom," says Curly, the leader of the gang. "We forgot."

"Boys, this is Johnnie Wilson. He's here to look at your old apartment."

"Oh, you're going to like it," says Curly. "It's a groovy apartment."

"There it is," says Blossom, pointing to apartment thirteen. She takes out her key and opens the door. "After you, Johnnie."

Johnnie enters the apartment. It's dark inside, with just one small light-bulb hanging from the ceiling. He looks around the room and his mouth drops open. Everything in the apartment is in bad condition; the furniture is broken, the walls have cracks, and the roof leaks. Johnnie looks down and sees a large bucket on the floor. It's full of water.

"Don't worry," says Blossom. "We're going to repair the roof."

"When?" asks Johnnie.

"Soon. Maybe this summer. Anyway, it's not a big problem."

"What?" says Johnnie.

Blossom smiles. "Look," she says, "the water only drips during the rainy season, and it only drips in the living room. The rest of the apartment is dry."

"I'm glad to know that," says John-nie. "Can I see the bedroom now?"

"Yes, of course," says Blossom. "Come with me." She leads Johnnie into the bedroom.

"The bed doesn't look very comfort-able," says Johnnie.

"Well, it is a little soft," says Blos-som. "But when you're tired, it doesn't make any difference."

"Why are the curtains closed?" asks Johnnie. "Are you trying to hide some-thing?"

"Not at all," says Blossom. "Do you want to see the view?"

"Please," says Johnnie.

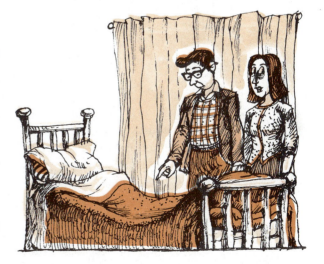

Blossom pulls back the curtains and Johnnie looks out the window. Across the street is a junk yard full of old, wrecked cars. Johnnie sees a big dog sitting on top of one of the cars. The dog looks like Brutus. Suddenly, Johnnie feels a sharp pain in his chest.

"Well, how do you like the apartment?" asks Blossom.

Johnnie is very polite. He doesn't like to criticize. "I don't think this is the right apartment for me," he says.

"Why not?"

"Well, four hundred dollars is a lot of money. I don't think I can afford to pay the rent."

"Why didn't you think of that before you came here?"

"Well, to be honest, this apartment isn't very good. In fact, it's terrible. I'm going to stay with my Uncle Ed. Good-bye."

"Wait a minute," says Blossom, looking very surprised. "Your uncle's name is Ed? Ed Wilson?"

"That's right. Why?"

Blossom sits down on the bed. "This is unbelievable," she says. "Ed Wilson is my old boyfriend. We were high school sweethearts."

"Oh, no, you're mistaken," says Johnnie. "It must be a different Ed Wilson. You see, my Uncle Ed is a bum. He never does anything."

"That's him!" cries Blossom, happily. "And you're his nephew. Isn't it a small world?" Johnnie tries to leave, but Blossom stops him. "You can't leave without giving me your address," she says, standing between Johnnie and the door. Johnnie looks very uncomfortable. "Come on, you can tell me," says Blossom, smiling sweetly.

"Oh, all right," says Johnnie. "It's one eighty-five Bond Street."

Blossom claps her hands. "I'm so happy," she says. "I can't wait to see Eddie again. I'm going to come and visit you."

"Oh, wonderful," says Johnnie, walking out of the apartment. "This sure is my lucky day."

f   *Answer the following questions about the story.*

1. When did Johnnie arrive at the Sherwood Oaks Apartments?
2. What is Blossom Blake like? Describe her. *She looks cheap, trashy, sleazy*
3. Why is Johnnie in a hurry to find an apartment?
4. Why does Blossom tell Johnnie, "This is your lucky day"? *She wants to convince him the apartment is a good bargain, good deal.*
5. What does Johnnie see at the end of the hallway?
6. What are the three men doing?
7. Why is Blossom unhappy? *She's embarrassed by the bums in the hallway.*
8. Who is the leader of the gang?
9. What does Curly say about their old apartment?
10. What is apartment thirteen really like? What's wrong with it?
11. Why isn't Blossom worried about the roof?
12. What does Johnnie see when he looks out the bedroom window?
13. What reason does Johnnie give for not taking the apartment?
14. What is the real reason he doesn't want the apartment? *Because it's a dump!*
15. Why is Blossom so happy when she finds out that Johnnie's uncle is Ed Wilson?
16. What happens when Johnnie tries to leave the apartment?
17. Why does Blossom want Johnnie's address?
18. Do you believe Johnnie when he says, "This sure is my lucky day"? *It's sarcastic*

Ed	Brutus	Johnnie

selfish   *mean*   *timid*

g   *What is your opinion of Ed, Brutus, and Johnnie? Describe them using some of the adjectives from the list below. Can you think of any other adjectives that are appropriate?*

polite ≠ rude	smart ≠ dumb	weak ≠ strong
generous ≠ selfish	happy ≠ unhappy	timid ≠ aggressive
loud ≠ quiet	harmless ≠ dangerous	neat ≠ sloppy
lazy ≠ hard-working	pleasant ≠ disgusting	mean ≠ gentle

h   *A week later, Blossom goes to visit Ed and Johnnie. Ed is very happy to see Blossom. He asks her for a date and she accepts. Write a short composition about their date. Where do they go? What do you think happens?*

i   *Answer the following questions.*

1. Is it easy or difficult to find an apartment in your city?
2. Describe your house or apartment.
3. What kind of furniture do you have in your living room?
4. Do you have a nice view? What can you see from your living room window?
5. Do you live near shopping and transportation? Are you in a good location?
6. Describe the street you live on. Is it wide or narrow? quiet or noisy?
7. What are your neighbors like? Are they friendly?
8. Do you know most of your neighbors? How often do you talk with them?
9. Do you like your neighbors? Why or why not?

j   *Make sentences using these adverbs of frequency:* **always, often, usually, sometimes, seldom, never.**

Example: take the bus
Student A: **How often do you take the bus?**
Student B: **I always take the bus.** OR **I seldom take the bus.**

1. drink coffee
2. make breakfast
3. walk to school
4. study at the library
5. talk about sports
6. listen to rock music
7. wear jeans
8. play cards
9. write letters
10. read the newspaper
11. watch TV
12. go to the movies

k   *Add sentences that explain or give a reason for the first sentence.*

Examples: Ed is a difficult person to live with. *He has a lot of bad habits.*
                                         OR *He's very selfish.*

          Can you loan me five dollars? *I'm broke.*
                                         OR *I need to buy some gas.*

1. I can't go to the movies with you tonight. _____

2. Anne doesn't like her job. _____

3. Mr. and Mrs. Golo are saving their money. _____

4. Barbara and Tino want to visit Paris. _____

5. We always eat at Mom's Cafe. _____

6. We like our neighbors. _____

7. My sister is very happy today. _____

8. I'm mad at my brother. _____

9. I can't talk to you now. _____

10. I'm tired. _____

1 *Ask and answer questions about the pictures, as indicated.*

1. A: **Do Mark and Diane want to get married?**
   B: **Yes, they do.**

   A: **Why?**
   B: **Because they're in love.**

2. A: **Does Albert want to play football?**
   B: **No, he doesn't.**

   A: **Why not?**
   B: **Because he's tired.**

3. Does Bob want to dance with Linda?

4. Does Linda want to ride on Bob's motorcycle?

5. Do the Golos want to eat at Maxim's?

6. Do Mr. and Mrs. Bascomb want to visit Canada?

7. Does Nick want to take a shower?

8. Do the Browns want to buy a clock?

m *Complete the following sentences using the affirmative or negative form of* **have to** + *verb.*

Examples: Our team (win) __*has to win*__ the football game. It's very important.

There's plenty of time, so we (hurry) *don't have to hurry*.

1. Gloria's car is at the garage. She (take) _____ _____ the bus to work.

2. She (get up) _____ early. Her job doesn't start until noon.

3. You (attend) _____ the meeting. It isn't necessary.

4. I (go) _____ now. My sister is waiting for me.

5. Jack has an easy life. He (work) _____ very hard.

6. His refrigerator is empty. He (go) _____ to the market.

7. You (make) _____ dinner. We can go to a restaurant.

8. We (stop) _____ at a gas station. There's hardly any gas in the tank.

9. Maria (cut) _____ her hair. It's getting too long.

10. She (use) _____ make up. She looks good without it.

11. I (clean up) _____ my apartment. It looks terrible.

12. You (help) _____ me. I can do it alone.

n *Complete the following sentences using* **a lot of, much, many, a few,** *and* **a little.**

Examples: Maria likes her coffee with a lot of cream but only __*a little*__ sugar.

There aren't __*many*__ cups on the shelf.

1. Mr. Bascomb is a busy man. He doesn't have __much__ free time.

2. He works hard and makes __a lot of__ money.

3. He knows a lot of people, but he doesn't have __many__ good friends.

4. There are only __a few__ people at the Martinoli Restaurant today.

5. Anne isn't very hungry. She's only having __a little__ soup for lunch.

6. Tino is very athletic and plays __many__ sports.

7. How __m__ sports can Barbara play?

8. Mrs. Golo has a lot of envelopes, but she has only __a few__ stamps.

9. How __much__ paper does she have?

It takes Barbara an hour to get ready for a date.

o   *Ask and answer questions as indicated.*

Example: walk to the market
Student A: **How long does it take you to walk to the market?**
Student B: **It takes me about five minutes.**

1. take a shower
2. wash your hair
3. get dressed
4. eat breakfast

5. make the bed
6. get ready for a date
7. walk to the post office
8. read the newspaper

9. write a letter
10. make a cup of coffee
11. brush your teeth
12. wash your clothes

p   *Complete the following sentences using these prepositions: **for, of, from, with, in, to.***

Example: My sister lives ___*with*___ her husband ___*in*___ New York.

1. Barbara is getting ready _____ her date _____ Tino.

2. He invited her _____ a movie.

3. Anne lives a long distance _____ her job.

4. She usually takes the bus _____ work.

5. The manager _____ our apartment building is very friendly.

6. He's nice _____ everyone.

7. Otis bought an expensive present _____ Gloria.

8. It was a bottle _____ perfume _____ France.

9. We're taking a trip _____ Mexico _____ June.

10. Mexico is famous _____ its beautiful beaches.

11. Can you help me _____ my homework?

12. I don't understand some _____ the exercises _____ this chapter.

q *Ask and answer questions as indicated. Use the present, past, and future tenses.*

Example 1:   tomorrow
Student A: **What are you going to do tomorrow?**
Student B: **I'm going to see a movie.**

Example 2:   last weekend
Student A: **What did you do last weekend?**
Student B: **I went to the beach.**

1. last night
2. this weekend
3. every morning
4. right now

5. after this class
6. yesterday
7. tonight
8. on weekends

9. last Sunday
10. today
11. in your free time
12. this Saturday

r *Complete the following sentences using suitable adjectives. There can be more than one suitable adjective for each sentence.*

Example: Barney told a *funny* story and everyone laughed.

1. Susie is very ___polite___ courteous. She always says "please" and "thank you."

2. Anyone can ride a bicycle. It's ___easy simple___.

3. Sam is ___tired___ exhausted 기진맥진. because he worked hard all day.   diligent

4. Ed is ___slacker___ bum =lazy. He never does any work.
   slug

5. Someone drank all the coke. The bottle is _____.

6. We have to hurry. We're ___late___ for the concert.

7. The concert is ___free___. We don't have to pay.

8. Maria is ___frustrated___ because she can't find her car keys.

9. The theater is only a ___short___ distance from here. We can walk.

10. There's no danger. The streets are ___safe___ in this neighborhood.

s *Add question tags to the following sentences.*

Examples: Mrs. Golo is a teacher
          Mrs. Golo is a teacher, isn't she?

          She doesn't work at the bank.
          She doesn't work at the bank, does she?

1. Johnnie lives with his Uncle Ed. doesn't he?
2. Ed is always broke.
3. He never has any money. does he?
4. He can't find a job. can he?
5. He took all of Johnnie's food. didn't he

6. He didn't leave anything. did he?
7. Johnnie is hungry. isn't he
8. The market isn't far. is it.
9. Johnnie can buy more food. can't he

t *Answer the following questions about yourself.*

1. Where did you go after class yesterday? What did you do?
2. Where did you eat dinner last night? What did you have? How was it?
3. Do you eat between meals? What is your favorite snack?
4. How often do you go to the market? What kind of food do you buy?
5. What programs do you watch on TV? What did you watch last night?
6. Did you sleep well last night? How many hours did you sleep?
7. What time did you get up this morning? What did you have for breakfast?
8. Do you normally take a shower in the morning? Do you ever sing in the shower?
9. Do you come from a large family? How many brothers and sisters do you have?

ONE STEP FURTHER

When Johnnie says to Blossom, ''This sure is my lucky day,'' he doesn't really mean it. This is an example of sarcasm: a person says one thing when he means exactly the opposite. We know that Johnnie doesn't feel lucky at all; he feels very unlucky because everything went wrong. People often use sarcasm when they are upset about something or when they want to be funny. Here are some more examples of sarcasm:
You lose your keys and say, ''That was smart of me.''
You know someone who is lazy and say to him, ''Don't work too hard.''

1. Can you give an example of sarcasm?
2. Do you think it's OK to use sarcasm?
3. Do you always know when someone is being sarcastic?
4. Do people often use sarcasm in your country?
5. Do you ever use sarcasm?

SKETCH

Select one student to be Johnnie. Select another student to be Ed.
Situation: Johnnie complains about Ed's bad habits. Ed tells Johnnie that he isn't perfect, either. Use some of the ideas in the story on pages 56–57 and some of your own ideas.

Select one student to be the manager of an apartment building. Select another student to be a person who wants to rent an apartment.
Situation 1: the manager shows the person an apartment that has a lot of things wrong with it. The person decides not to rent the apartment. Use some of the ideas in the story on pages 60–62 and some of your own ideas.
Situation 2: the manager shows the person an apartment that is in beautiful condition. The person is very happy and decides to rent the apartment.

COMPOSITION

1. Write about a day when everything went right.
2. Write about a day when everything went wrong.
3. Describe your neighbors. What are they like?

VOCABULARY

advertisement	dark	hard-working	neat	soon
affirmatively	date (n.)	harmless	nephew	straight
afford	difficult	hate	neighborhood	suddenly
aggressive	dining table	hide		surprised
air-conditioning	disgusting	honest	own	sweetheart
angrily	drip			sweetly
anyway	dumb	ignore	paint (n.)	
attitude		include	parking	tenant
available	electricity	included	point (v.)	timid
	end	inside	polite	T-shirt
bongos	excellent		pool	
breathe		junk yard	pull back	unbelievable
broken	feel			uncomfortable
	frown	knock	rent (n.)	unfurnished
carpet	furnished		rent (v.)	unemployed
ceiling		laundry	rude	unhappy
chest	gang	lead	selfish	utilities
circle	generous	leader	share	
clap	gentle	leak (n.)	sharp	view
close	glad	location	shave	
complain	groovy		shopping	wrecked
condition		manager	situation	
crack (n.)	habit	maybe	sloppy	yell
criticize	hallway	mean	sofa	
curtain	hang	middle-aged		
cry				

EXPRESSIONS

He's broke.
He has a bad attitude.
That's the way he likes it.
What can he do about it?

This is your lucky day.
It doesn't make any difference.
Isn't it a small world?
I can't wait to see Eddie.

I'm moving out.
I can't afford to pay.
You sure got here fast.
What can I do for you?

Come on.
After you.
That's right.
You're mistaken.

Take a look.
from now on
not at all

TEST

1. Sam is very popular.
   He has _____ friends.

   A. much   C. a few
   B. a lot of   D. any

2. Mr. Bascomb is a busy man.
   He doesn't have _____ free time.

   A. much   C. some
   B. many   D. no

3. We need some matches. We don't have

   _____.

   A. much   C. any
   B. some   D. none

4. Barbara likes her coffee with _____
   sugar.

   A. much   C. a few
   B. many   D. a little

5. Hurry up! The show starts in _____
   minutes.

   A. many   C. a few
   B. much   D. a lot of

6. There aren't _____ people in the
   theater.

   A. many   C. some
   B. much   D. no

7. Peter enjoys his work _____ it's
   interesting.

   A. although   C. so
   B. because   D. but

8. It was warm and sunny yesterday,
   _____ I went to the beach.

   A. although   C. so
   B. because   D. but

9. Barney borrowed some money
   _____ the bank last month.

   A. for   C. to
   B. of   D. from

10. He thanked Mr. Bascomb _____ his
    help.

    A. for   C. to
    B. of   D. from

11. We're taking our vacation _____
    August.

    A. for   C. on
    B. at   D. in

12. Nancy is going _____ France next
    year.

    A. in   C. at
    B. to   D. on

13. Johnnie lives _____ Bond Street.

    A. at   C. on
    B. in   D. to

14. I usually have lunch _____ one
    o'clock.

    A. at   C. on
    B. in   D. from

15. Those aren't your magazines.
    Don't take _____.

    A. they   C. this
    B. them   D. that

16. Here's my phone number. You can call
    _____ at home.

    A. I   C. mine
    B. my   D. me

17. Where's your brother? I have to talk
    with _____.

    A. he   C. him
    B. her   D. them

18. _____ did Mr. Wankie sell his car?
    Because he needed the money.

    A. How   C. Where
    B. Why   D. When

19. _____ did Linda go home?
    At three o'clock.

    A. When   C. Why
    B. Where   D. How

20. _____ does Mrs. Hamby work?
    At the post office.

    A. How   C. When
    B. Why   D. Where

21. _____ pencil do you want, the red one or the blue one?

    A. Whose   C. Which
    B. What   D. Who's

22. Jane doesn't have _____ in her handbag.

    A. something   C. nothing
    B. anything   D. none

23. Our club is having a big party Saturday night. _____ is going.

    A. Someone   C. Everyone
    B. Anyone   D. Every person

24. Jimmy can't go _____ this afternoon. He has to do his homework.

    A. nowhere   C. somewhere
    B. everywhere   D. anywhere

25. I like Jimmy and Linda. They're _____ good friends of mine.

    A. both   C. either
    B. all   D. neither

26. Ed ate all the cookies. There are _____ left.

    A. nothing   C. some
    B. none   D. any

27. We all make mistakes. Nobody's _____.

    A. perfect   C. good
    B. wonderful   D. fine

28. People usually speak _____ in the library.

    A. quiet   C. soft
    B. loudly   D. softly

29. Mr. Bascomb can't see very _____ without his glasses.

    A. good   C. well
    B. perfect   D. fine

30. Put on your coat. It's _____ outside.

    A. hot   C. warm
    B. cold   D. sunny

31. I have to do _____ homework.

    A. my   C. mine
    B. me   D. many

32. The Golos are painting _____ kitchen.

    A. there   C. their
    B. they're   D. theirs

33. We're taking the typewriter because it's _____.

    A. yours   C. our
    B. theirs   D. ours

34. Gloria says those envelopes are _____.

    A. her   C. our
    B. hers   D. your

35. Listen! Someone _____.

    A. come   C. is coming
    B. comes   D. are coming

36. The refrigerator is empty. We _____ go to the market.

    A. has to   C. like to
    B. have to   D. needs to

37. Where are the boys?
    They _____ in the park.

    A. play   C. is playing
    B. plays   D. are playing

38. I never _____ a hat.

    A. wear   C. am wearing
    B. wears   D. is wearing

39. Barney _____ to a movie yesterday.

    A. go   C. is going
    B. goes   D. went

40. Does Peter drive a sports car?
    Yes, he _____.

    A. do   C. drive
    B. does   D. drives

41. Did Maria work last Saturday?
    No, she _____.

    A. did   C. didn't work
    B. didn't   D. not work

42. You don't have much free time,
    _____?

    A. don't you   C. you do
    B. you don't   D. do you

43. It's a beautiful day, _____?

    A. it's not   C. isn't it
    B. it is   D. it isn't

44. Your apartment is close to everything.
    You live in a good _____.

    A. situation   C. location
    B. condition   D. station

45. Sam worked very hard. He must be
    _____.

    A. tired   C. polite
    B. weak   D. lazy

46. Anne has a lot of problems.

    A. Practice makes perfect.
    B. That's nice of her.
    C. That sounds like fun.
    D. That's too bad.

47. She doesn't like to work for Mr. Bas-
    comb. She thinks he's a bad _____.

    A. boss   C. employee
    B. owner   D. customer

48. The _____ for this apartment is
    three hundred dollars a month.

    A. price   C. bill
    B. rent   D. pay

49. Ed doesn't have any money. He's
    _____.

    A. broke   C. wrecked
    B. broken   D. middle-aged

50. London is the capital of England, isn't
    it?

    A. You're mistaken.
    B. It's a small world.
    C. That's right.
    D. Not at all.

CHAPTER FIVE

Future with "will"   **Would like a . . .**
Shall (suggestions and offers) Would like to . . .

a

b

a Mrs. Brown planned to go to the market today. She wanted to get some steak for dinner because it's on sale this week. However, she decided to stay home and clean the house. She'll go to the market tomorrow. At the moment, Mrs. Brown is resting. She's very tired after all the housework she did today.

1. Where did Mrs. Brown plan to go today?
2. Why did she want to get steak for dinner?
3. What did Mrs. Brown decide to do?
4. When will she go to the market?
5. What do you think she'll get?
6. What is Mrs. Brown doing at the moment?
7. Why is she tired?

b Tino is very fond of Barbara and often buys her presents. However, this week he was very busy and didn't buy her anything. Perhaps he'll give her something next week. Right now Barbara and Tino are walking to the bus stop. Barbara wants to stop and look at some hats. But Tino is in a hurry. He's afraid they'll miss the bus.

1. Does Tino often buy presents for Barbara?
2. Did he buy her anything this week?
3. Why not?
4. Do you think he'll give her something next week?
5. What do you think he'll give her?
6. Where are Barbara and Tino going now?
7. Why is Tino in a hurry?

AFFIRMATIVE

She'll go to the market tomorrow.
He'll _____.
I'll _____.
You'll _____.
We'll _____.
They'll _____.

She will go to the market tomorrow.
He will _____.
I will _____.
You will _____.
We will _____.
They will _____.

c *Make affirmative sentences with* **will**.

    Example: Mrs. Brown didn't go to the market today.   (tomorrow)
        She'll go to the market tomorrow.

1. Peter didn't call Maria last night.   (tonight)
2. He didn't go to the office today.   (tomorrow)
3. Linda didn't see Albert yesterday.   (on Saturday)
4. They didn't have a party this week.   (next week)
5. Jimmy didn't do his homework today.   (tomorrow)
6. Mrs. Golo didn't make dinner last night.   (tonight)
7. She didn't feed the cat yesterday.   (today)
8. I didn't wash the car this week.   (next week)
9. Nancy didn't visit Paris last March.   (in June)

BARBARA: Hello. I'm looking for a summer dress.

SALESLADY: I'll show you our cotton dresses.

BARBARA: This one's very nice.

SALESLADY: And it's only fifteen dollars.

BARBARA: Good. I'll take it.

SALESLADY: I'll put it in a box for you.

JACK GRUBB: Can you come to our club meeting tonight, Sam?

SAM BROWN: I'm sorry, I won't have the time. I'll come next week.

JACK GRUBB: You won't forget, will you?

SAM BROWN: No, I won't forget.

d *Ask and answer questions about the pictures, as indicated.*

1. A: **Will Barbara buy the dress?**
   B: **Yes, she will.**

   A: **Why?**
   B: **Because she really likes it.**

2. A: **Will Joe get rich?**
   B: **No, he won't.**

   A: **Why not?**
   B: **He doesn't have any customers.**

3. Will Ed help Johnnie?

4. Will Brutus eat all the hot dogs?

5. Will Albert catch the bus?

6. Will Maria dance with Peter?

7. Will Mr. Bascomb give his money to the bandit?

8. Will Marty pass the test?

ALBERT: Are you having your party tonight?

LINDA: Yes, but there won't be any music.

ALBERT: Shall I bring my record player?

LINDA: Yes. Please bring it.

OFFERS

Shall I make some coffee?
_____ tea?
_____ soup?
_____ sandwiches?

a   *Make sentences with shall I.*

Examples: The phone is ringing.   (answer/phone)   We don't have any milk.   (get/milk)
           Shall I answer the phone?   **Shall I get some milk?**

1. Someone is at the door.   (open/door)
2. It's very hot today.   (make/lemonade)
3. The dog is hungry.   (feed/dog)
4. There isn't any dog food left.   (buy/dog food)
5. Some guests are coming this weekend.   (clean/house)
6. The grass is very long.   (cut/grass)
7. The car is dirty.   (wash/car)
8. There's a lot of noise outside.   (close/window)
9. Mrs. Golo is sick.   (call/doctor)

MR. GOLO:	What's for dinner, dear?
MRS. GOLO:	I didn't make anything.

MR. GOLO:	Shall we go to a restaurant?
MRS. GOLO:	Yes. That's a good idea.

SUGGESTIONS

Shall we go to a restaurant?
_____ coffee shop?
_____ cafeteria?
_____ snack bar?

b *Make sentences with **shall we.***

Examples: It's a beautiful day. (go/park)   I'm thirsty. (buy/drinks)
          Shall we go to the park?   **Shall we buy some drinks?**

1. This city has a famous museum.   (visit/museum)
2. The Student Club is having a meeting today.   (attend/meeting)
3. Let's go out tonight.   (go/movies)
4. I'm hungry. (have/dinner)
5. There isn't any food in the refrigerator.   (buy/food)
6. The market is closed.   (eat/Martinoli Restaurant)
7. It's a long distance from here.   (call/taxi)
8. Taxis are very expensive.   (take/bus)
9. There'll be a lot of people at the restaurant tonight.   (make/reservations)

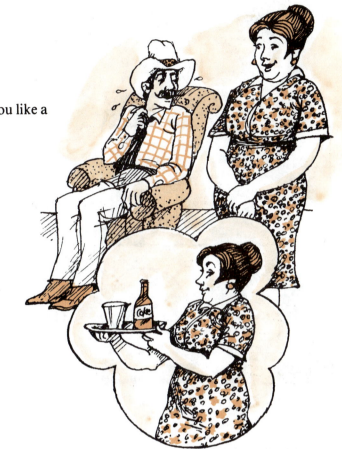

MABEL: You look thirsty, Sam. Would you like a drink?

SAM: Yes, I would.

MABEL: What would you like?

SAM: I'd like a Coke.

MABEL: OK, I'll get it for you.

SAM: Thank you, Mabel.

Would you like a glass of water?
_____ cup of coffee?
_____ bowl of soup?
_____ dish of ice cream?

c *Make sentences with* **would you like a . . . ?**

Example: I'm thirsty. (a glass of orange juice)
    Would you like a glass of orange juice?

1. It's very hot today. (a cold drink)
2. I'm hungry. (a sandwich)
3. I love lemonade. (a glass of lemonade)
4. Ice cream is my favorite dessert. (a dish of ice cream)
5. I'm thirsty. (a cup of coffee)
6. I don't like coffee. (a cup of tea)
7. My birthday is next week. (a shirt)
8. I have a lot of shirts. (a tie)
9. I have a lot of ties. (a hat)

TINO: Would you like to see a movie, Barbara?

BARBARA: No, I went to the movies last night.

TINO: Would you like to go to a dance?

BARBARA: No, not really.

TINO: What would you like to do then?

BARBARA: I'd like to stay home and watch television.

d *Ask and answer questions using* **would like to.** *Include some of the suggestions and alternatives listed below.*

STUDENT A: Would you like to see a movie, _____?
                            go dancing
                            play tennis
                            go to the park
                            visit the museum
                            go for a ride
                            take a walk
                            go swimming

STUDENT B: No, not really.

STUDENT A: What would you like to do?

STUDENT B: I'd like to go home and watch TV.
                            get some rest.
                            read a book.
                            sit by the fire.
                            write some letters.
                            play the piano.
                            listen to records.
                            look at some magazines.

Mr. and Mrs. Bascomb would like to visit Europe this summer. At the moment, they're talking to their travel agent, Mr. Winkle.

"We have three European tours," he says. "Our Grand Tour will be perfect for you. Would you like to see our brochure?"

"Yes, we would," says Mr. Bascomb. "These pictures are lovely. Will the tour include all of Europe, Mr. Winkle?"

"Of course. And you'll have a lot of free time in each country."

"I'd like to know more about the hotels," says Mrs. Bascomb. "Are they first class?"

"Naturally. You'll stay in the best hotels in Europe. They all have great locations, excellent rooms, and fine cuisine."

"Tell us more about the food," says Mr. Bascomb. "We like to eat well."

"You'll be happy to know all the restaurants on the Grand Tour are famous for their cuisine," says Mr. Winkle. "You can dine when and where you like, even in your room. At no extra charge."

"What about tipping?" asks Mrs. Bascomb. "Is the service included?"

"You don't have to worry about tipping," says Mr. Winkle. "The tour manager pays all the waiters, drivers, and guides."

"Can the tour manager translate for us?" asks Mr. Bascomb. "We don't speak any foreign languages."

"All the tour managers speak several languages. They can help you with anything you need."

"That's wonderful. What do you think, Henrietta? Shall we go?"

"Sure. We can take the tour in June."

"Shall I make your reservations now?" asks Mr. Winkle.

"Yes. Would you like a deposit?"

"Yes, thank you. That will be $200. I know you'll enjoy your trip."

a *Answer the following questions about the story.*

1. What would Mr. and Mrs. Bascomb like to do this summer?
2. Who are they talking to right now?
3. How many European tours does Mr. Winkle have?
4. Which tour does he think will be perfect for the Bascombs?
5. Will the Grand Tour include all of Europe?
6. Will they have much free time in each country?
7. Will they stay in first-class or second-class hotels?
8. What do the best hotels have?
9. Do all the tour members have to eat together at the same time?
10. Is it necessary to tip the waiters, drivers, and guides?
11. Do the Bascombs need a translator? Why?
12. When would Mrs. Bascomb like to take the tour?
13. Will Mr. Winkle make their reservations today?
14. How much is the deposit?

Barney Field is also going to Europe this summer. He doesn't have much money, so he is travel-ing on a two-week budget tour.

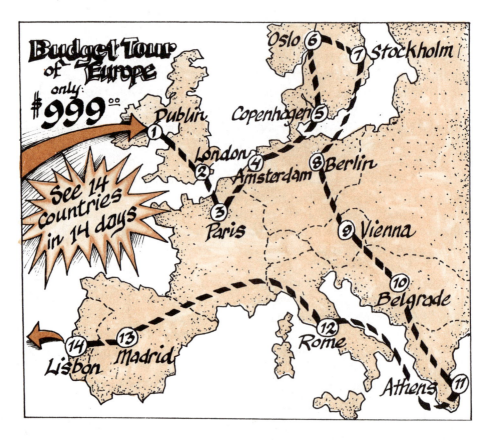

b *Work in pairs. Ask where Barney will be on each day of his trip and answer by looking at the map.*

Example: 1   Dublin
Student A: **Where will he be on the first day?**
Student B: **He'll be in Dublin.**

c   *Add question tags to the following sentences.*

Examples: You're coming to the meeting tonight.   You won't forget.
           You're coming to the meeting tonight, aren't you?   **You won't forget, will you?**

1. Barney repaired his car.
2. It wasn't very difficult.
3. Tino is getting something for Barbara.
4. It won't be anything expensive.
5. There's some food in the refrigerator.

6. We don't have to go to the market.
7. Maria can bring some food.
8. She's coming at eight o'clock.
9. You're going to call her.

d   *Make sentences with expressions of time.*

Examples: The meeting was at 10 o'clock.

Nancy arrived at 9:45.
She was 15 minutes early.

The Bascombs arrived at 10:12.
They were 12 minutes late.

I arrived at 10:00.
I was on time.

1. Barney arrived at 10:05.
2. The Browns arrived at 9:52.
3. Miss Jones arrived at 10:00.
4. We arrived at 10:20.
5. Maria arrived at 9:30.

6. Peter arrived at 9:45.
7. His friends arrived at 10:00.
8. Mrs. Golo arrived at 10:15.
9. You arrived at 10:30.
10. Barbara arrived at 9:50.

e   *Find the opposites and fill in the blanks.*

short	slow	boring	lose
never	easy	dry	forget
empty	sell	narrow	frown

1. difficult   *easy*
2. remember _____
3. always _____
4. interesting _____

5. fast _____
6. win _____
7. long _____
8. wet _____

9. buy _____
10. wide _____
11. full _____
12. smile _____

f   *Answer the following questions.*

1. What time will this class end? What are you going to do after class?
2. What will the weather be like tomorrow? Do you think it will be sunny or cloudy? What will the high temperature be?
3. What kind of weather do you like? Do you prefer the weather in summer or in winter?
4. What kind of clothes do you like to wear? Describe your favorite article of clothing.
5. Do you like to shop? Where are some good places to shop for clothes?
6. What would you like to do this weekend? this summer? next year?
7. Would you like to live in another city? If so, which one?
8. Where do you think you'll be a year from now?
9. What are your plans for the future?
10. What do you hope will happen this year or next year?

WAITRESS: Good evening. What would you like for dinner?

OTIS: I'll have spaghetti.

WAITRESS: Would you like soup or salad with your dinner?

OTIS: I'd like onion soup.

WAITRESS: Certainly. Anything to drink?

OTIS: Some iced tea, please.

WAITRESS: Yes, sir.

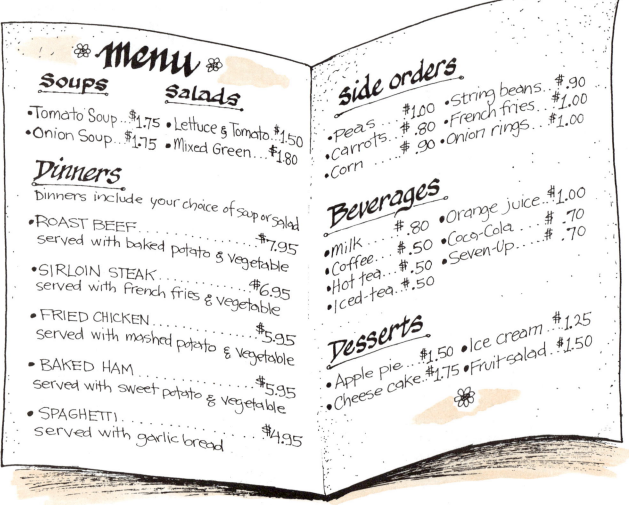

❀ Menu ❀

Soups
- Tomato Soup... $1.75
- Onion Soup... $1.75

Salads
- Lettuce & Tomato $1.50
- Mixed Green... $1.80

Dinners
Dinners include your choice of soup or salad

- ROAST BEEF.................... $7.95
  served with baked potato & vegetable

- SIRLOIN STEAK................ $6.95
  served with french fries & vegetable

- FRIED CHICKEN............... $5.95
  served with mashed potato & vegetable

- BAKED HAM.................... $5.95
  served with sweet potato & vegetable

- SPAGHETTI..................... $4.95
  served with garlic bread

Side orders
- Peas $1.00
- Carrots... $.80
- Corn
- String beans.. $.90
- French fries... $1.00
- Onion rings... $1.00

Beverages
- Milk.... $.80
- Coffee... $.50
- Hot tea... $.50
- Iced-tea.. $.50
- Orange juice... $1.00
- Coca-Cola.... $.70
- Seven-Up..... $.70

Desserts
- Apple pie... $1.50
- Cheese cake.. $1.75
- Ice cream... $1.25
- Fruit salad. $1.50

g   *Work in pairs. Practice ordering from the menu. After the first conversation, exchange roles.*

ONE STEP FURTHER

Mr. and Mrs. Bascomb are planning a European vacation.

1. Where would you like to spend your next vacation?
2. What would you like to do there?
3. Who would you like to go with?
4. How long would you like to stay?

SKETCH

Select one student to be a travel agent. Select another student to be a customer.
Situation 1: the customer has a lot of money and wants to take a deluxe tour. The travel agent recommends a special tour for rich travelers.
Situation 2: the customer has very little money. The travel agent recommends an inexpensive tour.

COMPOSITION

1. Describe your ideal vacation.
2. Write about your plans for the future.
3. Describe your favorite article of clothing. What color is it? What is it made of? Was it a present, did you buy it, or did someone make it for you? Do you wear it only on special occasions?

VOCABULARY

begin	dine	ideal (adj.)	reservation	tipping
brochure	distance			translate
budget	drink (n.)	lady	service	tour (n.)
			several	travel agent
cafeteria	even	naturally	shall	
cotton		next	shirt	will (v.)
cuisine	grand		steak	
	guide	own (v.)		
dance (n.)				
deposit (n.)	housework	present (n.)		

EXPRESSIONS

He's fond of her.	not really	first class
What's for dinner?	no extra charge	

PRONUNCIATION

θ

think	toothpaste	bath
thank	something	both
third	anything	fourth
thought	birthday	month

Both theaters are on Third Avenue.
I think he'll buy something on Thursday.

ð

that	these	another
them	those	weather
there	father	together
they	mother	neither

They saw their father and mother.
The other brother wasn't there.

My birthday is on the third Thursday of this month.
Those boys told the truth about everything.
They thanked both of their parents.

Future with WILL
Affirmative

He She I You We They	'll (will)	come tomorrow.

Negative

He She I You We They	won't (will not)	come tomorrow.

Interrogative

Will	he she I you we they	come tomorrow?

Short Answers

Yes,	he she I you we they	will.

No,	he she I you we they	won't.

OFFERS AND SUGGESTIONS

Shall	I	make some coffee?
	we	go to the movies?

Question with WOULD

Would you	like a	glass of water? cup of tea?
	like to	dance? play tennis?

Short Answer

Yes, I would.	No, I wouldn't.

CHAPTER SIX

Object pronouns   Too/enough
Phrasal verbs

a

A.   B.

b

A.   B.

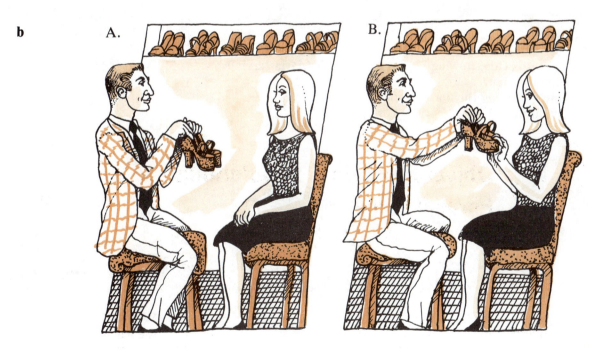

a A. Anne is bringing Mr. Bascomb some coffee. She's going to pour him a cup.

   B. Now she's pouring it for him. Mr. Bascomb is smiling at her. He always enjoys a cup of coffee in the morning.

1. What's Anne bringing Mr. Bascomb? (A)
2. What's she going to do?
3. What's she doing now? (B)
4. Do you think Mr. Bascomb is happy?
5. What does he enjoy in the morning?

b A. Barbara is in the Wickam Department Store. The salesman is showing Barbara some shoes.

   B. Now he's handing them to her. Barbara likes the shoes very much. She wants to try them on.

1. Where is Barbara? (A)
2. What is the salesman showing her?
3. What's he doing now? (B)
4. Does Barbara like the shoes?
5. What does she want to do?

VERBS WITH TWO OBJECTS

What is she bringing Mr. Bascomb?
_____ Mrs. Hamby?
_____ you and me?
_____ the women?

She's bringing him some coffee.
_____ her _____.
_____ us _____.
_____ them _____.

c *Ask and answer questions about the pictures. as indicated.*

1. A: **What is Otis showing the children?**
   B: **He's showing them a painting.**

2. What is Maria serving her guests?

She's serving them tea.
She is serving it to them

3. What is Peter buying Maria?

He is buying her some flowers.
He's buying them for her.

4. What is Linda feeding the rabbit?

She's feeding him a carrot
" it to him

5. What is Albert bringing Linda?

6. What is Susie giving the teacher?

She's giving it to him

MR. BASCOMB: Miss Jones, can I see you for a minute?

ANNE JONES: Of course, Mr. Bascomb.

MR. BASCOMB: Take these forms to Mr. Korn, please.

ANNE JONES: Yes, sir. I'll take them to him now.

JACK GRUBB: What are you doing, Sam?

SAM BROWN: I'm making a table for Mabel.

JACK GRUBB: When will you give it to her?

SAM BROWN: I'll give it to her this Sunday.

VERBS WITH TWO OBJECTS

He'll give the table to Mabel.   He'll give it to her.
_____ Jimmy.   _____ him.
_____ you and me.   _____ us.
_____ the Golos.   _____ them.

d *Change the following sentences, as indicated.*

Examples: Anne will take <u>the forms</u> to <u>Mr. Korn</u>.   He's getting <u>the TV</u> for <u>you and me</u>.
       She'll take <u>them</u> to <u>him</u>.   **He's getting <u>it</u> for <u>us</u>.**

1. Tino will buy <u>the hat</u> for <u>Barbara</u>.
2. She'll give <u>the magazines</u> to <u>you and me</u>.
3. I'll take <u>the lamp</u> to <u>the Browns</u>.
4. Jimmy is showing <u>the photographs</u> to <u>his girlfriend</u>.
5. Mabel is buying <u>the umbrella</u> for <u>Sam</u>.
6. Mrs. Golo is getting <u>the dictionary</u> for <u>her students</u>.
7. Johnnie sold <u>the books</u> to <u>Maria</u>.
8. We showed <u>the painting</u> to <u>our friends</u>.
9. Linda got <u>the records</u> for <u>Albert</u>.

e *Ask and answer questions about the pictures, as indicated.*

1. some wood, a hammer, and nails
A: **What can you *do* with some wood, a hammer, and nails?**
B: **You can *make* a table.**

2. some paper, string, and two pieces of wood

3. some lettuce, tomatoes, onions, and carrots

4. some lemons, water, and sugar

5. some bread, ham, and cheese

6. some chocolate, flour, and eggs

Barney <u>met</u> an old friend yesterday.

He <u>ran into</u> him on Oak Street.

People <u>respect</u> Dr. Pasto.

They <u>look up to</u> him because of his great knowledge.

The famous lawyer, Justin Case, is <u>defending</u> a client.

He's <u>standing up for</u> him in court.

Mr. Bascomb was very sick, but he <u>recovered</u> from his illness.

He <u>got over</u> it and went back to work yesterday.

PHRASAL VERBS (INSEPARABLE)

We looked for Maria at the hospital.
___ waited for _____.
___ called on _____.
___ ran into _____.

We looked for her at the hospital.
___ waited for _____.
___ called on _____.
___ ran into _____.

f   *Answer the following questions as indicated.*

Examples: Did Mr. Bascomb recover from his illness?   (get over it/last Monday)
   Yes, he got over it last Monday.

Did Barbara arrive late to work?   (turn up/an hour late)
Yes, she turned up an hour late.   *intransitive.*

1. Did Mr. Case defend that man?   (stand up for him/in court)
2. Did Barney meet an old friend yesterday?   (run into him/on Oak Street)
3. Did the old man chase those children?   (run after them/in the park)
4. Did Mabel return from the market?   (come back/on the bus)
5. Did Sam enter the restaurant with a woman?   (come in/with his wife)
6. Did Linda leave the house last night?   (go out with/Albert)
7. Did Jimmy finish his homework yesterday?   (get through/all of it)
8. Did Gloria leave the office?   (get off/at five o'clock)
9. Did Mr. Bascomb study those reports?   (go over them/at home)

Mr. Bascomb postponed his
meeting with Peter.

I don't feel well, Peter. Let's have our meeting next week instead of this week.

He put it off until the following
week.

Barbara got a package yesterday.

She picked it up at the post office.

Fred is considering a job at the post
office.

He's thinking it over very carefully.

Fred is refusing the job.

He's turning it down because he
doesn't like the hours.

PHRASAL VERBS (SEPARABLE)

Mr. Korn is going to look over those forms.
_____ fill in _____.
_____ take back _____.
_____ hand in _____.

He's going to look them over.
_____ fill them in.
_____ take them back.
_____ hand them in.

g   *Answer the following questions as indicated.*

Examples: Tino is going to call Barbara.   (ask _____ out tonight)
           He's going to ask her out tonight.

           Anne is going to learn Spanish.   (take _it__ up next summer)
           She's going to take it up next summer.

1. Mr. Korn is going to complete those forms.   (fill _them_ in this afternoon)
2. Anne is going to get a package at the post office.   (pick _it_ up in a few minutes)
3. Barney is going to repay Mr. Bascomb.   (pay _____ back next month)
4. He's going to repair his taxi.   (fix _it_ up this weekend)
5. Nancy is going to visit some friends at the hotel.   (look _____ up tomorrow)
6. I'm going to consider your offer.   (think _____ over this week)
7. Peter is going to study some business reports.   (look _____ over this afternoon)
8. He's going to meet Maria at the hospital.   (pick _____ up at six o'clock)
9. Mrs. Golo is going to return those books to the library.   (take _____ back today)

a

b

a Mrs. Golo is having lunch at the Wickam Restaurant. She doesn't think it's a very good place to eat. The waiter brought her too many potatoes and not enough meat. And her coffee is too hot to drink. Mrs. Golo is saying something to the waiter, but he can't hear anything. The music in the restaurant is too loud.

1. Where is Mrs. Golo having lunch?
2. Does she think it's a good place to eat?
3. Did the waiter bring her enough potatoes?
4. What about meat?
5. Why can't Mrs. Golo drink her coffee?
6. Is she saying something to the waiter?
7. Why can't he hear her?

b Johnnie is in the Wickam Department Store. He's trying on a new suit. He's unhappy because it doesn't fit him. The jacket is too small and the pants aren't long enough. Johnnie would like to buy his clothes at a more fashionable place, like the Continental Men's Shop. But it's expensive there and Johnnie doesn't have enough money this month.

1. Where's Johnnie?
2. What's he trying on?
3. Why is he unhappy?
4. Is the jacket the right size for Johnnie?
5. What about the pants?
6. Where would Johnnie like to buy his clothes?
7. Why doesn't he go to the Continental Men's Shop?

TOO AND ENOUGH

The jacket is too small.
_____ short.
_____ dark.
_____ old-fashioned.

It isn't big enough.
_____ long _____.
_____ light _____.
_____ fashionable _____.

c *Make sentences with too + adjective.*

Examples: That suit isn't big enough for Johnnie.
            It's too small.

            Sam doesn't have enough time to go to the movies.
            He's too busy.

1. Jimmy isn't old enough to drive a car.
2. Albert isn't tall enough to play basketball.
3. Linda isn't strong enough to lift those boxes.
4. Peter's car isn't big enough for five people.
5. Jack doesn't have enough money to buy a new car.
6. He doesn't have enough energy to clean his apartment.
7. Mr. Bascomb doesn't have enough time to play the piano.
8. It isn't hot enough to go to the beach.
9. That coat isn't heavy enough to wear in winter.

SUSIE: Are you trying to pick some oranges, Marty?

MARTY: I can't reach them, Susie. I'm not tall enough.

SUSIE: It isn't worth it. They look too green.

MARTY: You're right. They probably aren't ripe enough to eat.

SUSIE: Why don't you buy some oranges at the market?

MARTY: I don't have any money.

SUSIE: I've got fifty cents. Is that enough?

MARTY: That's enough to buy a whole bag of oranges. Let's go.

TOO

Marty is too short to pick the oranges.
_____ tired _____.
_____ lazy _____.

d *Make sentences with **too**.*

Example: Barbara is very tired. She can't play tennis.
She's too tired to play tennis.

1. Marty is very small. He can't play football.
2. Jimmy is very young. He can't drive a car.
3. Linda is very tired. She can't do her homework.
4. Maria is very busy. She can't go out with Peter tonight.
5. Jack is lazy. He won't get up at 6 o'clock.
6. Mr. Golo is sick. He can't get out of bed.
7. Alice is very young. She doesn't understand.
8. Mrs. Hamby is very fat. She can't wear that dress.
9. Johnnie is weak. He can't lift that table.

ENOUGH

Marty doesn't have enough money to go to the market.
_____ time _____.
_____ energy _____.

e *Make sentences with **enough**.*

Examples: Marty isn't very tall. He can't reach the oranges.
He isn't tall <u>enough</u> to reach the oranges.

He doesn't have much money. He can't buy oranges at the market.
He doesn't have <u>enough</u> money to buy oranges at the market.

1. Sam doesn't have much time. He can't help Linda with her homework.
2. Jimmy isn't very hungry. He can't finish his dinner.
3. Anne doesn't eat much. She won't get fat.
4. She isn't very strong. She can't lift those boxes.
5. Jack doesn't make much money. He can't buy a new car.
6. Peter's car isn't very big. It won't hold more than four people.
7. Albert isn't very tall. He can't play on the basketball team.
8. Mr. Golo isn't very well. He can't go to work.
9. Fred isn't very intelligent. He won't find a good job.

It's twelve-thirty. There's a hold-up at the City Bank. One of the bandits is pointing a gun at Miss Jones. She's very frightened. "Give me all the large bills," he says. "Do you want them in a bag?" "No. Just hand them to me. And don't try to call for help." "I'm not dumb enough to do anything like that," says Miss Jones.

Another bandit is giving orders to Mr. Bascomb. "Take me to the safe," he says. "And then open it for me."

"All right," says Mr. Bascomb. "But there's hardly anything in it." He's very worried. He hopes the police will come soon.

A third bandit is standing at the entrance to the bank. He's calling to his friends. "Let's go. We don't have much time. The police will be here in a few minutes."

a   *Answer the following questions about the story.*

1. What time is it?
2. What's happening at the City Bank?
3. Why is Anne frightened?
4. What does the bandit say to her?
5. Why doesn't she call for help?
6. What does the second bandit say to Mr. Bascomb?
7. Is there much money in the safe?
8. What does Mr. Bascomb hope will happen?
9. Where is the third bandit?
10. Why is he calling to his friends?

b   *Respond to the following sentences, as indicated.*

Examples: Three bandits held up the City Bank.   (the police / find)
Don't worry. The police will find them.

The phone is ringing.   (I / answer)
Don't worry. I'll answer it.

Mabel didn't buy any food today.   (Sam / get)
Don't worry. Sam will get some.

1. There isn't any milk left.   (we / buy)
2. Linda doesn't want her potatoes.   (Albert / eat)
3. The dishes are dirty.   (Jimmy / wash)
4. The cat is hungry.   (Mrs. Golo / feed)
5. There aren't any envelopes in the desk.   (I / get)
6. Maria lost her handbag.   (she / find)
7. Barney doesn't know about the party tomorrow night.   (Nancy / tell)
8. We can't walk to the party. It's too far.   (Peter / take)
9. Anne has a problem. She can't dance.   (I / teach)

c   *Answer the following questions using adverbs of frequency.*

Examples: Are you always hungry?   **Yes, I'm always hungry.**
                        OR   **No, I'm seldom hungry.**

Do you ever make dinner?   **Yes, I often make dinner.**
                        OR   **No, I never make dinner.**

1. Do you often go to the market?
2. Do you ever make lunch?
3. Are you always busy?
4. Are you usually in a hurry?
5. Do you always have fun?
6. Are you often tired?
7. Do you ever sleep late?
8. Are you sometimes late to class?
9. Do you usually put things off?
10. Do you often lose things?
11. Do you ever borrow money?
12. Do you sometimes loan money to your friends?

d   *Ask and answer questions about the pictures using* ***too*** *and* ***enough.***

1. A: Why can't Johnnie lift the chair?

   B: He isn't strong <u>enough</u>.
      OR   **The chair is <u>too</u> heavy for him.**

2. A: Why can't Jimmy drink beer?

   B: He's <u>too</u> young.
      OR   **He isn't old <u>enough</u>.**

3. Why isn't Albert enjoying the party?

4. Why can't Fred hear Barney?

5. Why can't Marty pick the oranges?

6. Why doesn't Johnnie like the jacket?

7. Why doesn't Mrs. Golo like her dinner?

8. Why doesn't Jack cut the grass?

e   *Change the following sentences using object pronouns.*

Examples: Turn on the light.
      Turn it on.

Look over those reports for me.
Look them over for me.

1. Fill out these forms.
2. Put on your coat.
3. Take back those books.
4. Pick up Maria at the hospital.
5. Give back that magazine.

6. Pay back Mr. Bascomb.
7. Look up my sister and me in Wickam City.
8. Turn off the light.
9. Take off your shoes.

f   *Complete the following sentences with suitable prepositions.*

Example: The salesgirl put the dress ___*in*___ a box ___*for*___ Barbara.

1. Johnnie has a lot _____ books _____ philosophy _____ his shop.

2. There are two books _____ Ken Killuga _____ the window.

3. Barbara likes her coffee _____ a little sugar _____ it.

4. "Come and see me _____ the bank _____ Monday," said Mr. Bascomb.

5. He put off his meeting _____ Peter _____ the following week.

6. All _____ the people _____ that room are friends _____ mine.

7. Linda recovered _____ her illness and went back _____ school yesterday.

8. Sam had a few cups _____ coffee _____ Jack _____ the snack bar.

9. Tino is getting a box _____ chocolates _____ Barbara _____ the candy shop

10. Peter is taking Maria _____ the movies _____ his sports car.

g   *Answer the following questions about yourself.*

1. Do you like to write letters? How long does it take you to write a letter?
2. Do you think there's enough time for everything? How do you find time for all the things you want to do?
3. What are your plans for this evening? Are you going to stay home or go out?
4. Are you saving your money to buy something? If so, what is it?
5. How far do you live from the market? Do you walk, drive, or take the bus to the market? How long does it take you to get there?
6. How much time do you spend on the phone? Who do you call? What do you talk about?
7. What time do you normally have dinner? How long does it take you to eat dinner?
8. How do you dress when you go to a party? What do you wear when you want to be comfortable?
9. Do you belong to a club? If so, what kind of club is it? When do you have your meetings? What kind of things do you do?

ONE STEP FURTHER

Three bandits held up the City Bank today.
1. Are there many hold-ups or robberies where you live?
2. What are some other common crimes?
3. What are the reasons for crime?
4. Why is there so much crime in big cities?
5. Does your city have a good police department?
6. How is it possible to reduce crime?

SKETCH

Select one student to be the owner of a store. Select another student to be a bandit.
Situation: the bandit tries to rob the store. The store owner says there is very little money in
   the cash register. He tries to stop the bandit. They have an argument.

Select one student to be Mrs. Golo. Select another student to be a waiter.
Situation: Mrs. Golo is having lunch at the Wickam Restaurant. She complains to the waiter
   about the food. The waiter can't hear Mrs. Golo very well because of the loud music.

Select one student to be Johnnie. Select another student to be a salesperson in a men's
   clothing store.
Situation: Johnnie is trying on a suit that is too small for him. He complains to the salesperson.
   The salesperson finds another suit, but this time Johnnie doesn't like the color.

COMPOSITION

1. Write about a famous robbery or hold-up. What did the robbers take? When and where did
   it happen? Did the police catch the robbers? How?
2. Write about your job. What kind of work do you do? Describe the things you like and don't
   like about your job.
3. Describe your dream house. What color is it? How many rooms does it have? What is the
   furniture like? Does it have a balcony? a fireplace? Is there a garden?

VOCABULARY

bag (n.)	defend	great (adj.)	offer (n.)	probably	strength
bandit	dumb				suit (n.)
		hand (v.)	package (n.)	reach (v.)	
catch (v.)	energy	happen	pants (n.)	recover	teach
client	enough (adj.)	hear	place (n.)	refuse (v.)	team (n.)
common (adj.)	enough (adv.)	heavy (adj.)	point (v.)	repay	tired (adj.)
consider	entrance	hold-up (n.)	police	respect (v.)	turn down
court (n.)			postpone	ripe	
	far (adj.)	illness	pour		whole (adj.)
	fashionable	instead		safe (n.)	worth
	feel (v.)				
	finish (v.)	jacket (n.)			
	fit (v.)				
	following (adj.)	knowledge			
	frighten				
		lawyer			
		light (n.)			

EXPRESSIONS

It isn't worth it.   hold-up   hardly anything   old-fashioned

PRONUNCIATION

a

fond	pocket	politics
blond	modern	philosophy
cotton	hospital	economy
concert	strong	belong

The doctor's blond daughter wants a job at
the hospital.
She's fond of hot dogs and pop songs.

ə

under	money	husband
truck	couple	company
public	lucky	trouble
come	number	construction

The young couple was in front of the truck.
Some hungry customers are coming from
the bus.

The public doesn't want another long, hot summer.
The rock concert continued until one o'clock.

WORD ORDER WITH DIRECT AND INDIRECT OBJECTS

Tom is	buying getting giving bringing	her him me you us them	the book.

He's	buying getting giving bringing	it	for to	her. him. me. you. us. them.

PHRASAL VERBS (INSEPARABLE)

We're	looking waiting	for	Maria. our friends.

We're	looking waiting	for	her. them.

PHRASAL VERBS (SEPARABLE)

He's	picking up putting away	the newspaper. the magazines.

He's	picking putting	the newspaper the magazines	up. away.

He's	picking it up. putting them away.

ENOUGH

That dress isn't	big long pretty	enough for Linda.

TOO

It's too	small. short. plain.

ENOUGH

Mrs. Golo doesn't have enough	time to go to the library. energy to clean the house. strength to lift that table.

TOO

She's too	busy (to go to the library). tired (to clean the house). weak (to lift that table).

CHAPTER SEVEN

Ago/how long ago?   **Past continuous**
Must (obligation)

a

b

a Mr. Brown left his shop at 5:30. Then he went to the barber shop. He arrived there at 5:45. That was 15 minutes ago. It's 6 o'clock now.

1. What time did Sam leave his shop?
2. What time did he arrive at the barber shop?
3. What time is it now?
4. How long ago did Sam leave his shop?
5. How long ago did he arrive at the barber shop?

b It's 9:15. Tino and Barbara would like to see a film called "Sweet Summer." They're looking at the cinema guide. The first show began at 7:15. The second show began at 9 o'clock.

1. What time is it?
2. What would Tino and Barbara like to see?
3. How long ago did the first show begin?
4. How long ago did the second show begin?
5. Is it too late to see the entire film?

AFFIRMATIVE

Sam left his shop fifteen minutes ago.
_____ half an hour ago.
_____ an hour ago.
_____ a long time ago.

c *Complete the following sentences with any suitable verb in the past tense. Add a preposition when necessary.*

Example: Sam *went to* the barber shop a little while ago.

Linda *finished* her homework half an hour ago.

1. Barney _____ his car a couple of weeks ago.

2. We _____ the museum a few weeks ago.

3. Mr. Bascomb _____ breakfast an hour ago.

4. He _____ the newspaper a little while ago.

5. He _____ the bank a few minutes ago.

6. Mrs. Golo _____ a bath an hour ago.

7. She _____ the dog fifteen minutes ago.

8. She _____ the dishes a long time ago.

9. Maria _____ a letter a few days ago.

10. She _____ the rent a week ago.

11. I _____ my brother a little while ago.

12. He _____ a haircut a few days ago.

MR. BASCOMB: Have you got a book called "Modern Banking"?

JOHNNIE WILSON: I sold the last copy two months ago.

MR. BASCOMB: Did you order more copies of the book?

JOHNNIE WILSON: Yes, I did.

MR. BASCOMB: How long ago did you order them?

JOHNNIE WILSON: About a week ago.

MRS. BROWN: Was Sam here today?

BARBER: Yes, he was. He came for a haircut.

MRS. BROWN: I must find him. Do you know where he went?

BARBER: Yes. I think he went to Nick's Garage. It's not far from here.

MRS. BROWN: How long ago did he leave?

BARBER: He left fifteen minutes ago. He must be there now.

d *It's twelve o'clock. Ask and answer questions about the pictures, as indicated.*

1. A: **How long ago did Barney get up?**
   B: **He got up three and a half hours ago.**

2. How long ago did he eat breakfast?

3. How long ago did Anne clean the kitchen?

4. How long ago did she read the newspaper?

5. How long ago did Otis call Gloria?

6. How long ago did he pick her up?

7. How long ago did they arrive at Mom's?

8. How long ago did they leave Mom's?

a

b

a Last night Albert visited the Brown family. When he arrived, Mr. Brown was writing letters and his wife was reading a book. Jimmy was watching television and Linda was talking on the phone.

1. Who did Albert visit last night?
2. What was Mr. Brown doing when he arrived?
3. What was Mrs. Brown doing?
4. What was Jimmy doing?
5. What was Linda doing?

b At eight o'clock this morning Tino was sleeping. At the same time, Barbara was waiting for the bus and Anne was having breakfast.

1. What was Tino doing at eight o'clock this morning?
2. What was Barbara doing while Tino was sleeping?
3. What was Anne doing while Barbara was waiting for the bus?
4. Was Tino sleeping while Barbara was waiting for the bus?

PAST CONTINUOUS

He was sleeping at eight o'clock.
_____ getting up _____.
_____ taking a shower _____.
_____ eating breakfast _____.

They were working this morning.
_____ studying _____.
_____ reading _____.
_____ writing_____.

c *Answer the following questions as indicated.*

Examples: What was Anne doing at eight o'clock?   (having breakfast)
   She was having breakfast.

   What were Nick and Barney doing this morning?   (working)
   They were working.

1. What was Barbara doing at eight o'clock?   (waiting for the bus)
2. What was she doing at ten o'clock?   (working at the bank)
3. What was she doing at one o'clock?   (having lunch with Tino)
4. What were Jimmy and his friends doing this morning?   (studying at the library)
5. What were they doing this afternoon?   (playing basketball)
6. What was Jack doing at the park yesterday?   (feeding the birds)
7. What was Peter doing at the hospital yesterday?   (visiting Maria)
8. What were the Browns doing last weekend?   (cleaning the house)
9. What were they doing last night?   (watching television)

ANNE: You have a nice boyfriend, Barbara.

BARBARA: Thank you. I'm glad you like him.

ANNE: Where did you meet Tino?

BARBARA: I was sitting in a cafe when I met him.

PAST CONTINUOUS

Barbara was sitting in a cafe when she met Tino.
_____ waiting _____.
_____ eating_____.
_____ having lunch _____.

d   *Answer the following questions as indicated.*

Example: What was Gloria doing when Otis called?   (washing her hair)
          She was washing her hair (when he called).

1. What was Mabel doing when Sam arrived?   (making dinner)
2. What was Jimmy doing when the telephone rang?   (studying)
3. What were the Browns doing when Albert came?   (watching television)
4. What were they doing when he left?   (playing cards)
5. What was Peter doing when the telegram arrived?   (reading a book)
6. What was Maria doing when he called?   (working at the hospital)
7. What was Mrs. Golo doing when the fire started?   (talking on the phone)
8. What was Mr. Golo doing when the fire started?   (listening to the radio)
9. What were they doing when the firemen arrived?   (standing in front of the house)

JACK: What did you do last night, Sam?

SAM: I wrote some letters. And you?

JACK: While you were writing letters,
        I was working at the snack bar.

SAM: Oh, really?

e   *Have similar conversations with other students.*

STUDENT A: What did you do last night/this morning, _____ ?

STUDENT B: I _____ . And you?

STUDENT A: While you were _____ , I was _____ .

STUDENT B: Oh, really?

Include some of the activities listed below.

listen to the radio	read a magazine
play cards	do my homework
watch television	have breakfast/dinner
work in the garden	take a walk in the park
talk on the phone	clean the house/apartment
play tennis	study at the library
work at the office	write some letters
watch the football game	dance at the Disco Club

A few months ago Peter Smith had an accident. He was driving to work
when a dog ran in front of his car. He turned sharply and missed the dog.
But his car hit a tree. A policeman was standing on the corner when the
accident happened. He called an ambulance immediately. The attendants
came and took Peter to the hospital. While they were driving to the
hospital, Peter was talking about the accident. "The dog caused the
accident," said Peter. "It wasn't my fault."

Peter Smith stayed in the hospital for a month. But he wasn't sad. While
he was in the hospital, Peter was planning his next trip to Europe. "I'm
going to visit France, and then go to Germany," he said. "Germany is
beautiful in the fall."

The nurse smiled. "That's wonderful," she said. "You're lucky you can
travel to so many interesting places."

a *Answer the following questions about the story.*

1. When did Peter have the accident?
2. Where was he going when the dog ran in front of his car?
3. Did Peter hit the dog?
4. Did he hit anything?
5. Who was standing on the corner when the accident happened?
6. What did he do?
7. Where did the attendants take Peter?
8. What was Peter talking about while they were driving to the hospital?
9. Was the accident Peter's fault?
10. How long did Peter stay in the hospital?
11. What was he thinking about while he was in the hospital?
12. What countries did Peter plan to visit?
13. Do you think Peter is lucky or unlucky?

b *Write an appropriate sentence for each road sign from the list below.*
Use each sentence only once.

You must stop.   You must keep to the right.   You must turn right.
You must not park.   You must not enter.   You must not make a U turn.
You must not turn left. You must turn left.

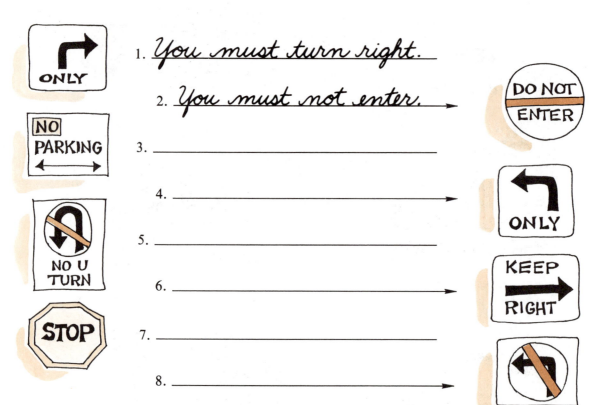

1. *You must turn right.*
2. *You must not enter.*
3. _____
4. _____
5. _____
6. _____
7. _____
8. _____

Must in the affirmative has almost the same meaning as **have to:**
   You must go = You have to go.

Must in the negative has the same meaning as a negative command:
   You must not go = Don't go.

c   *The people on this page were all doing different things last Saturday afternoon.*
Ask and answer questions about the pictures using the past continuous.

Mabel

A: **What was Mabel doing?**
B: **She was sewing a sweater.**

Otis and Gloria

A: **What were Otis and Gloria doing?**
B: **They were riding their bicycles.**

Albert and Linda

Jack Grubb

Sam and Jimmy

Maria

Fred

The boys

d *Write questions with **who, what,** or **where**.*

Examples: Barbara was waiting for the bus. *What was she waiting for?*

She was talking to Anne. *Who was she talking to?*

They were going to the museum. *Where were they going?*

1. Otis and Gloria were having lunch at Mom's Cafe. _____

2. Gloria was wearing a green dress. _____

3. They were talking about Dr. Pasto. _____

4. Sam was writing a letter to his brother. _____

5. Mabel was cleaning the kitchen. _____

6. Albert and Linda were studying at the library. _____

7. They were listening to the radio. _____

8. Nancy was talking to Barney on the phone. _____

9. The boys were playing football in the park. _____

e *Ask and answer questions as indicated.*

Example: The policeman was standing on the corner when the accident happened.
Student A: **What was the policeman doing when the accident happened?**
Student B: **He was standing on the corner.**

1. Nancy was washing the dishes when Barney arrived.
2. Sam was reading a book when the telephone rang.
3. The girls were watching television when Maria left.
4. Barbara was looking at the menu when Tino called the waiter.
5. Jack was looking for a seat when the play started.
6. He was sleeping when the play ended.
7. The ladies were playing cards when Dr. Pasto came.
8. Linda was having breakfast when Albert brought the package.
9. Jimmy was watching her when she opened the package.
10. They were listening to records when Mabel entered the room.

f *Ask and answer questions using the past continuous.*

Example: this morning at ten o'clock
Student A: **What were you doing this morning at ten o'clock?**
Student B: **I was walking to the library. OR I was reading a book.**

1. this morning at eight o'clock
2. last night at seven o'clock
3. last night at ten-thirty
4. at this time yesterday
5. at noon yesterday
6. at this time last year

g   *Ask and answer questions as indicated.*

Example: ride a bicycle
Student A: **When was the last time you rode a bicycle?**
Student B: **The last time was about ten years ago.**
                OR   I rode a bicycle two weeks ago.

1. write a letter
2. read a good book
3. go to a movie

4. eat in a restaurant
5. take a vacation
6. play basketball

7. go to a party
8. lose something
9. have an accident

h   *Complete the following sentences using these adverbs: **safely, slowly, hard, quickly, beautifully, easily, loudly, peacefully, immediately, dangerously, softly**. Use each adverb only once.*

Example: Nancy walks ___*quickly*___ . She's always in a hurry.

1. Mr. and Mrs. Holt spoke _____ because their daughter was sleeping.

2. When the doctor found out the baby was sick, he came _____ .

3. It takes Anne a long time to type a letter. She types very _____ .

4. We complained because some people were talking _____ in the theater.

5. Natalya and Boris dance _____ together because they practice all the time.

6. I won't go anywhere with Jack because he drives _____ .

7. Mr. Poole was worried about the children, but they returned home _____ .

8. My sister has a quiet life. She lives _____ in a small town in the country.

9. If you want to be successful, you have to work _____ .

10. This exercise isn't difficult. You can do it _____ .

i   *Answer the following questions about yourself.*

1. Are you getting together with anyone tonight or tomorrow? What do you plan to do?
2. Do you like to dance? Do you know a good place for dancing?
3. Do you like to sing? What's your favorite song?
4. When was the last time you went to a party? What did you do at the party?
5. Do you think it's important to be on time? When was the last time you were late for something? Why were you late?
6. What did you do yesterday morning? yesterday afternoon?
7. How often do you go to the movies? When was the last time you saw a good movie? What was it about?
8. How often do you write letters? Who do you write to? Can you write a letter in English?
9. How often do you speak English outside of class? How many of your friends speak English?

ONE STEP FURTHER

Peter had an automobile accident. He says that it wasn't his fault.
1. Who do you think was responsible for the accident?
2. Do you think most people are good drivers?
3. What are some reasons for car accidents?

Barbara was sitting in a cafe when she met Tino.
1. Do you remember when you met an important person in your life?
2. Where were you?
3. What were you doing?
4. What was he or she doing?

SKETCH

Select one student to be the driver of an automobile. Select another student to be his friend.
Situation: the driver had an accident recently. His friend wants to know when and where
    the accident took place and how it happened.

Select one student to be a salesperson in a department store. Select another student to be a
    customer.
Situation: the customer is looking for a birthday present for a friend or relative but doesn't know
    what to get. The customer asks the salesperson for help. The salesperson asks who the
    present is for and then makes some suggestions.

COMPOSITION

1. The automobile is an important means of transportation in the United States. Describe
    the different means of transportation in your country.
2. Write about an accident you had or about an accident you saw.
3. Write about a time when you helped someone or someone helped you. Was the person
    a stranger or a friend?
4. Write about a party you went to recently. Was it a special occasion?

VOCABULARY

accident	daily	hit (v.)	sharply
ago (adv.)			sweater
ambulance	entire	must	sweet (adj.)
attendant			
automobile	fault (n.)	ride (v.)	telephone number
	front		
barber (n.)		seat (n.)	while (conj.)
	glad	sew	while (n.)
cause (v.)			
cinema			
copy (n.)			

EXPRESSIONS

I'm glad.   It wasn't my fault.

PRONUNCIATION

b

busy	Cuban	umbrella
bandit	handbag	library
banana	about	club
borrow	nobody	cab

Mabel's husband is buying a black umbrella.
Nobody borrows money from that bank.
Barney wants bread and butter for breakfast.

v

vase	clever	drive
very	never	love
visit	lovely	leave
vegetable	envelope	shave

They have a very expensive vase.
The clever visitor is leaving the university.
Marvin never shaves in the evening.

Leave the brown envelopes on the table.
Barney never buys vegetables or bananas.
The lovely ballet dancer waved goodbye to the clever bandit.

Interrogative

How long ago	did the movie start? did they leave?

Affirmative

It started They left	a few minutes ago. a little while ago. half an hour ago.

HAVE TO

He She	has to	get up early.
I You We They	have to	go to the market. buy some food.

MUST

He She I You We They	must	get up early. go to the market. buy some food.

PAST CONTINUOUS   **Affirmative**

He She I	was	sleeping working	when the telephone rang.
You We They	were	reading studying	while it was raining.

Negative

He She I	wasn't (was not)	sleeping working	when the telephone rang.
You We They	weren't (were not)	reading studying	while it was raining.

Interrogative

Was	he she I	sleeping? working?
Were	you we they	reading? studying?

Short Answers

Yes,	he she I	was.
	you we they	were.

No,	he she I	wasn't.
	you we they	weren't.

CHAPTER EIGHT

Review

Yesterday Sam Brown was talking to a visitor when Albert came into the room.

"Mr. Brown," he said, "I have to talk with you."

"Of course, Albert. Would you like some hot chocolate and cake?"

"Yes, thank you Mr. Brown." Albert was breathing hard. "I heard that you're going to sell your house and move to a farm in the country. Is it true?"

"Yes, it is, Albert. I was just talking to Mr. Fix about it. He's the real estate agent. We were looking at some photos of farmland and . . . "

"But Mr. Brown, why are you selling your house and moving away?" Albert looked very unhappy.

"Well, Albert, Wickam City is getting too big for me. There are too many people in this town, and there isn't enough room to breathe. Besides, Mabel and I always wanted to live on a farm."

Just then Mabel came into the room. She was carrying a large tray full of lemonade, hot chocolate, cookies, homemade candy, and cake.

"Hello, Albert," she said. "It's nice to see you. We have lemonade and hot chocolate. Which would you prefer?"

"I'll have both, thank you," said Albert. He was very hungry, as usual.

"And you, Mr. Fix?" she said. Mabel was a good hostess and always thought of her guests.

"Neither one for me," he said. "I don't want any."

Mr. Fix looked at Albert. Albert was drinking lemonade while balancing a cup of hot chocolate on his right knee and a plate full of cake and cookies on his left knee.

"You must be very thirsty," he said.

"I am," said Albert. He finished all of the lemonade and then drank the hot chocolate. After that he picked up a piece of cake.

"I made a lot of cake," said Mabel, "so eat all you want."

"I will," said Albert.

"Okay," said Mr. Fix. "But I never eat much before dinner."

"I'm afraid the cookies aren't very good this time," said Mabel. "I left them in the oven too long and they're a little dry."

"That's okay, I'll eat them anyway," said Albert, taking another handful.

"Oh Mabel," laughed Sam, "you're just looking for compliments. Everything tastes pretty good to me."

"I guess I will have a little cake," said Mr. Fix. "And now Mr. Brown, let's talk business. I have two pieces of property here. One has a lot of land, with fruit trees and animals on it. But there aren't any towns nearby. The only town in the area is Colterville, and it's about fifty miles away. The other piece of property is quite small and doesn't have any fruit trees or animals, but it's close to town. Which one would you like?"

"Well," said Sam, "Mabel and I were talking it over and we decided to take the first piece of property, the one that's a long way from town, with the animals and fruit trees."

"That's right, Mr. Fix," said Mabel. "It looks so peaceful there."

"When will the farm be available?" asked Sam.

"In about three weeks."

Just then Albert coughed. Everyone turned and looked at him.

"Why Albert," cried Mabel. "You ate all the cake and cookies."

"That's incredible," said Mr. Fix. "I didn't think it was possible."

"You aren't making a very good impression," said Sam. He was disappointed in Albert.

"I'm sorry," said Albert. "But Mr. and Mrs. Brown, you can't move to the country."

"Why not, Albert?" asked Mabel.

"I think I know," said Sam, smiling. "Don't worry, Albert. Linda is still going to the University. She'll stay here and live with the Golos. You can see her whenever you want."

"Well, that's nice," said Albert. "There's something else, though."

"What's that, Albert?" asked Mabel.

"If you move to the country, I can't eat here anymore," replied Albert, reaching for another piece of candy. "I'm sure going to miss your cooking, Mrs. Brown."

a *Answer the following questions about the story.*

1. Who was Sam talking to when Albert came into the room?
2. What were they looking at?
3. Why does Sam want to leave Wickam City and move to a farm?
4. Who came into the room while Sam was talking to Albert?
5. What was she carrying on her tray?
6. Did Albert want lemonade or hot chocolate?
7. What did Mr. Fix want?
8. How many pieces of property does Mr. Fix have?
9. What's the first piece of property like?
10. What's the second one like?
11. Which piece of property did Sam and Mabel decide to take?
12. Why is Albert unhappy that the Browns are leaving Wickam City?
13. Where is Linda going to live?
14. Would you like to live on a farm? Why or why not?

b *Make sentences using **must be** + adjective.*

Examples: Albert is eating a lot.   Anyone can learn to type.
        He must be hungry.   **It must be easy.**

1. Everyone wants to read that book.
2. It takes a long time to learn Russian.
3. Dr. Pasto can discuss anything.
4. People think Barbara looks like a movie star.
5. Fred always makes the same mistake.
6. Mrs. Hamby has to wear very large clothes.
7. Tino has a good job and a beautiful girlfriend.
8. The Martinoli Restaurant always has a lot of customers.
9. Mr. Bascomb doesn't have time for anything.

c   *Complete the following sentences using the past continuous and the past simple.*

Examples: Sam (talk) *was talking* to a visitor when Albert (arrive) *arrived* .

We (walk) *were walking* home when we (hear) *heard* a loud noise.

1. The passengers (sleep) _____ when the plane (land) _____ .

2. Peter (drive) _____ to work when he (have) _____ an accident.

3. Anne (work) _____ at the bank when the telegram (arrive) _____ .

4. Otis and Gloria (take) _____ their seats when the movie (start) _____ .

5. Daisy (clean) _____ the kitchen when Simon (appear) _____ at the door.

6. Sam (make) _____ breakfast when Mabel (get up) _____ this morning.

7. They (have) _____ a conversation when Jimmy (enter) _____ the room.

8. We (play) _____ cards when our friends (call) _____ .

9. Nancy (take) _____ a shower when the phone (ring) _____ .

10. Mr. Hamby (travel) _____ in Mexico when he (get) _____ sick.

11. Gloria (wash) _____ the dishes when she (drop) _____ the plate.

12. I (do) _____ my homework when you (turn on) _____ the radio.

d   *Make sentences using **both, neither, all,** and **none.***

Examples: Both of those languages are easy.   None of my friends are lazy.
            Neither of them is difficult.   **All of them are energetic.**

1. Neither of those men is strong.
2. Both of those women are rich.
3. All of those magazines are old.
4. None of those oranges are ripe.
5. All of these glasses are clean.

6. Neither of these dresses is long.
7. None of my friends are stupid.
8. All of them are happy.
9. Both of those cars are slow.

e   *Ask and answer questions using the past tense.*

Example: take my magazine
Student A: **Did you take my magazine?**
Student B: **No, I didn't. Someone else took your magazine.**

1. eat my sandwich
2. drink my coke
3. take my money

4. clean the kitchen
5. open the window
6. drop the vase

7. write that letter
8. borrow my dictionary
9. use my shampoo

f *Complete the following dialogue using* **some, someone, something, somewhere, any, anyone, anything,** *and* **anywhere.**

ANNE: I hear a noise. Is there ___*someone*___ in the kitchen?

NANCY: No, there isn't _____ in the kitchen. But I think there's

_____ at the door.

MARIA: You're right. It's Barney. He wants to ask you _____.

BARNEY: Hello, Nancy. I need _____ stamps. Can I borrow

_____ from you?

NANCY: Sure, Barney. Is there _____ else?

BARNEY: Yes, does _____ here know _____ about

Swiss watches?

ANNE: I don't know _____ about watches, but I think

Switzerland is _____ in Europe.

BARNEY: Very funny. Look, there's _____ wrong with my watch. Do

you know where I can take it for repairs?

MARIA: There aren't _____ watch repair shops around here. Maybe you

can find a shop _____ downtown.

BARNEY: Hmm, that gives me an idea. Are you ladies going _____ this

afternoon?

NANCY: We don't have _____ plans. Why?

BARNEY: My taxi is outside. We can all go downtown and look for a watch repair shop

together. After that, I'll take you _____ for lunch.

NANCY: That's a great idea, Barney. We accept your invitation.

NANCY: Hi, Barney. We're having a picnic this Saturday. Would you like to come?

BARNEY: Oh, I'd like to, but I can't. I have to take my sister to the airport.

NANCY: That's too bad. It's going to be a a great picnic.

BARNEY: Well, maybe next time. Thanks anyway.

g   *Have similar conversations. Student A invites Student B to a social event, such as a picnic or a party. Student B declines the invitation and gives an excuse for not going. Here are some possible excuses:*

I have to study for an exam.
_____ do some shopping.
_____ clean the house/apartment.
_____ help my father/mother.
_____ do my homework.

_____ go to a meeting.
_____ work at the office.
_____ do some laundry.
_____ get ready for a trip.
_____ go out of town.

h   *Make sentences using phrasal verbs with object pronouns.*

Examples: Tino wants to listen to the radio.   (turn on)
He's turning it on now.

Mrs. Golo borrowed some books from the library last week.   (take back)
She's taking them back now.

1. Barbara got a new typewriter today.   (try out)
2. Peter received some business reports a little while ago.   (look over)
3. Barney borrowed some money from Mr. Bascomb a few days ago.   (pay back)
4. Mr. and Mrs. Golo have a problem.   (talk over)
5. Linda took some books from the living room.   (put back)
6. Nancy wants the telephone number of the post office.   (look up)
7. Anne is taking her coat from the closet.   (put on)
8. Mr. Poole left his children at the park.   (pick up)
9. Jack turned on the light in the bedroom.   (turn off)

i   *Answer the following questions about yourself using phrasal verbs.*

1. When you don't know the meaning of a word, where do you look it up?
2. When you have a problem, who do you talk it over with?
3. When was the last time you ran into an old friend?
4. How often do you go out on week nights?
5. How often do you go away on the weekends?
6. When was the last time you turned down an invitation?
7. When was the last time you put off a meeting?
8. What sport(s) would you like to take up?
9. What famous person do you look up to?

Wickam City is an average-sized town in California. It's not far from the mountains, and it takes only a few minutes to drive to the ocean. The weather is excellent, with a lot of sunshine and only a few days of rain during the winter months. It hardly ever snows in the city, but there is plenty of snow in the mountains from December to April.

The residents of Wickam City are lucky in many respects. They have clean air, and there isn't much traffic or noise. Public transportation is very good. A lot of people take the bus to work and some even ride their bicycles. Wickam City has many pleasant, uncrowded streets. And there is almost no pollution. That's because there isn't much industry, just an old ice cream factory on Clark Street.

Although Wickam City doesn't have much green space, there is a beautiful park on the east side called City Park. It's a popular place for picnics and family outings. People in Wickam City really enjoy nature and try to take advantage of the natural beauty that surrounds them. At certain times of the year, during the late fall and spring months, it's possible to ski in the mountains and swim in the ocean, all in the same day.

The mountains and beaches are excellent tourist attractions. However, there isn't much tourism in Wickam City because the town has only a few first-class hotels. Most visitors stay at the Wickam Hotel on Third Avenue.

Wickam City has a good police department and there is very little crime. It's true there was a hold-up at the City Bank a few weeks ago, but the police found the robbers and returned all the money. Mr. Bascomb was very happy about that.

Wickam City has a lot of entertainment, and everyone likes to go out and have a good time. There are a lot of theaters and restaurants in the downtown area, and they are usually filled with people on the weekends. Unfortunately, there aren't many nightclubs or discotheques in town. The only good place for dancing is the Disco Club on Rock Street.

People in Wickam City love sports and are very proud of their football team, the Wickam Warriors. There is also a lot of interest in music and the arts. This month they are having an important exhibition at the Art Museum, featuring paintings by famous European artists, including Picasso. In the summer, people enjoy concerts at the open-air theater in City Park. The Symphony Orchestra gives a lot of free performances there.

Ordinarily residents of Wickam City are not very interested in politics, but this is an election year. The current mayor, Frank Connors, is retiring after eight years in office. The people will vote for a new mayor this fall. So far, the only candidate for the job is John Bascomb, president of City Bank.

j   *Answer the following questions about Wickam City.*

1. What state is Wickam City in?
2. Is it far from the mountains?
3. How long does it take to drive to the ocean?
4. How is the weather in Wickam City?
5. What is public transportation like?
6. How much traffic and noise is there?
7. Why isn't there much pollution in Wickam City?
8. Why isn't there much tourism?
9. Where do most visitors stay?
10. How much crime is there in Wickam City?
11. Did the police catch the men who held up the City Bank?
12. What did the police do with the money?
13. What kind of entertainment does Wickam City have?
14. Is there much interest in music and the arts?
15. What about politics?
16. Why are people interested in politics this year?

k   *Ask and answer questions about each other's home towns, as indicated.*

Examples: parks
Student A: **Are there many parks in your home town?**
Student B: **(No, there aren't many, only a few, very few, etc.)**
              (No, there aren't any, there are none, etc.)

              tourism
Student A: **Is there much tourism in your home town?**
Student B: **Yes, there's a lot of tourism in my home town.**
              (No, there isn't much, only a little, very little, etc.)
              (No, there isn't any, there's none, etc.)

1. banks
2. office buildings
3. factories
4. industry
5. unemployment
6. crime

7. hotels
8. restaurants
9. nightclubs
10. traffic
11. noise
12. pollution

13. parks
14. libraries
15. theaters
16. tourism
17. entertainment
18. interest in sports

l   *Add question tags to the following sentences.*

Examples: Wickam City has a good police department.
              Wickam City has a good police department, doesn't it?

              There isn't much crime.
              There isn't much crime, is there?

1. There isn't much traffic in Wickham City.
2. A lot of people take the bus.
3. There was a hold-up at the City Bank.
4. The police found the robbers.
5. Most people aren't interested in politics.
6. Mr. Bascomb is the only candidate for mayor.
7. The Browns are moving to the country.
8. They don't like Wickam City.
9. Sam was talking to the real estate agent.

m *Answer the following questions about your home town.*

1. Where is your home town?
2. What is the weather like in your home town?
3. What kind of public transportation is there?
4. What kind of entertainment is there?
5. What kind of tourist attractions are there?
6. What are the streets and houses like in your home town?
7. What are the people like?
8. What are some things you like about your home town?
9. What are some things you don't like?

n *Complete the following sentences with suitable prepositions.*

Example: Mabel came ___*into*___ the room ___*with*___ a tray full ___*of*___ cake and cookies.

1. Same wants to live _____ a farm _____ the country.

2. One _____ the farms is close _____ town and the other is far _____ town.

3. Wickam City is half an hour _____ the ocean _____ bus.

4. There's plenty _____ snow _____ the mountains _____ December _____ April.

5. Most visitors stay _____ the Wickam Hotel _____ Third Avenue.

6. There are a lot _____ concerts _____ the open-air theater _____ City Park.

7. Linda's going _____ the beach _____ Albert today.

8. Mr. Bascomb is having a bowl _____ soup _____ lunch.

9. I'm giving my father a book _____ animals _____ his birthday.

o *What do you think is going to happen in these situations? Make sentences using **going to**.*

Example: Anne is walking to the post office. **She's going to mail a letter.**
                                                                 OR She's going to buy some stamps.

1. Linda is tired.
2. Albert is hungry.
3. Nancy has a headache.
4. Barney's clothes are dirty.
5. Mabel is going to the market.
6. Fred needs some money.
7. Maria is looking for the shampoo.
8. Tino is picking up the phone.
9. The girls are looking at the cinema guide.
10. The sky is full of black clouds.

p   *Make sentences with would you like to . . . ?*

Examples: It's a beautiful day for tennis. (play)   Dogs are wonderful pets. (have)
               Would you like to play tennis?   **Would you like to have a dog?**

1. France is a beautiful country. (visit)
2. Volkswagens are good cars. (own)
3. Spanish is an important language. (learn)
4. Movie stars are interesting. (meet)
5. New York is a great city. (live)
6. I like Los Angeles. (work)
7. It's a nice day for the beach. (go)
8. My favorite store is having a sale on beach balls (buy)
9. I need some money. (borrow)

q   *Complete the following sentences in your own words.*

Examples: I'm too tired *to play tennis/to make dinner.*

             She's smart enough *to go to college/to become a doctor.*

1. He's hungry enough _____
2. She isn't old enough _____
3. It's too hot _____
4. We're too late _____
5. Do you have enough money _____
6. I don't have enough time _____
7. They're too busy _____
8. He's too lazy _____
9. She isn't strong enough _____

r   *Look at the picture on page 137. Ask for and give directions as indicated.*

Example 1:   barber shop → Olson's Department Store
Student A: **Excuse me. How can I get to Olson's Department Store from here?**
Student B: **Go to Main Street, turn right, go (up) one block to Star Avenue and you'll see it across the street.**

Example 2:   Rex Theater → drug store
Student A: **Excuse me. How can I get to the drug store from here?**
Student B: **Go (down) two blocks to Lime Street, turn left and you'll see it next to the church.**

1. drug store → post office
2. bookstore → City Park
3. flower shop → Rex Theater
4. post office → State Bank
5. parking lot → gas station
6. Mom's Cafe → bookstore
7. Grand Hotel → barber shop
8. supermarket → post office
9. Rex Theater → flower shop
10. gas station → Mom's Cafe
11. barber shop → Grand Hotel
12. church → Olson's Department Store

BOB: Hello. Can I speak to Linda, please?

SAM: Linda isn't here. Can I take a message?

BOB: Yes, tell her that Bob called.

SAM: Does she have your number?

BOB: I think so, but I'll give it to you anyway. It's 265-0378.

SAM: Okay, I'll tell her you called.

s   *Have similar conversations. Student A calls Student B and leaves a message for a friend.*

t   *Make suggestions using "Why don't you . . . ?"*

Example:
Student A: **I'm bored.**
Student B: **Why don't you call your friends?**
            OR   **Why don't you go to a movie?**

1. I'm thirsty.
2. I'm hungry.
3. I'm broke.
4. I'm lonely.
5. I'm tired.

6. It's cold in here.
7. The roof is leaking.
8. The windows are dirty.
9. There's no food in the refrigerator.
10. I need some stamps.

u   *Answer the following questions using object pronouns.*

Examples: Did Mr. Bascomb loan the money to that woman?
            Yes, he loaned it to her.

            Did Gloria show her pictures to Otis?
            Yes, she showed them to him.

1. Did Mabel give the yellow lamp to the Golos?
2. Did Barbara take the magazines to Mr. Bascomb?
3. Did he send the package to his wife?
4. Did Mrs. Golo show the new dictionary to the students?
5. Did Johnnie sell the books to Dr. Pasto?
6. Did Sam give the table to Mabel?
7. Did he give the dog to Jimmy and Linda?
8. Did they show the dog to Albert?
9. Did Tino send the flowers to Barbara?
10. Did she loan the record player to her friends?

v   *Answer the following questions about shopping at the market.*

1. How often do you go to the market?
2. Which market is your favorite? How far is it from your house?
3. What hours is the market open?
4. How long does it take you to do the shopping?
5. Do you ever have to wait in long lines?
6. What kind of food do you buy?
7. Does the market usually have what you're looking for?
8. Are the fruit and vegetables always fresh?
9. Are the employees friendly? helpful? courteous?
10. What do you like about your market? What don't you like?

ONE STEP FURTHER

Most residents of Wickam City think it's a great town.
1. What are some of the things you like about your home town? What are some things you don't like?
2. Give a physical description of your home town. What are the houses and streets like? What's the weather like?
3. Describe the public transportation in your home town.
4. Describe the tourist attractions in your home town.
5. What's the entertainment like in your home town? Where do people like to go at night?

SKETCH

Select one student to be Linda. Select another student to be Albert.
Situation: Linda asks Albert if he can recommend a good movie. Albert tells Linda about a new movie that is playing at the Rex Theater. They decide to go and see it.

CONVERSATION PRACTICE

Pairs of students discuss their home town(s).

COMPOSITION

1. Describe your home town. How big is it? Is it near the ocean or the mountains? What are the houses and streets like? Are there many parks? Where is the business district?
2. Describe the tourist attractions or the entertainment in your home town.
3. Tell why you like or don't like your home town.
4. Write about an interesting day. What happened to you? Where were you? Who were you with?

VOCABULARY

accept
advantage
almost
anticipation
area
attraction
available
average-sized

balance (v.)
beauty

candidate
certain
cooking
cough (v.)
crime

current (adj.)

dancing
disappointed

east (adj.)
election
energetic
entertainment
excellent

farmland
feature (v.)

green space

handful
homemade
home town
hostess

if
impression
incredible
industry
interest (n.)
interest (v.)
invitation

knee (n.)

land (n.)
left (adj.)

mayor

natural
nature

open-air
ordinarily
outing (n.)
oven

peaceful
performance
photo
plenty
pollution

possible
property
proud

real estate
respect (n.)
retire

ski (v.)
snow (n.)
snow (v.)
stadium
state (n.)
station (n.)
sunshine

surrounded
Swiss

taste (v.)
though
tourism
traffic (n.)
tray

uncrowded

vote (v.)

EXPRESSIONS

so far   in many respects   to take advantage of   to make a good impression

TEST

1. _____ people take the bus.
   - A. Much
   - B. A little
   - C. A lot of
   - D. Any

2. They don't have _____ clothes.
   - A. much
   - B. some
   - C. few
   - D. many

3. There's _____ milk in the refrigerator.
   - A. a little
   - B. much
   - C. a few
   - D. many

4. They need some envelopes.

   They don't have _____.
   - A. some
   - B. any
   - C. a few
   - D. much

5. There wasn't _____ traffic on that street last night.
   - A. many
   - B. some
   - C. a little
   - D. much

6. I'm only going to buy _____ stamps.
   - A. many
   - B. much
   - C. a few
   - D. a little

7. Linda _____ go to the market today.
   - A. have to
   - B. has to
   - C. need to
   - D. likes to

8. Nancy _____ speak French.
   - A. can to
   - B. wants
   - C. want to
   - D. can

9. Albert is hungry. He _____ to have dinner now.
   - A. can
   - B. want
   - C. wants
   - D. likes

10. My friends _____ to play tennis.
    - A. like
    - B. wants
    - C. can
    - D. likes

11. Both of those men are tall.

    _____ of them is short.
    - A. None
    - B. Neither
    - C. All
    - D. Some

12. Maria has two radios. _____ of them are good.
    - A. Some
    - B. All
    - C. Both
    - D. One

13. Dr. Pasto has a lot of books.

    _____ of them are very old.
    - A. Some
    - B. Any
    - C. Neither
    - D. Both

14. All of those oranges are ripe.

    _____ of them are green.
    - A. Some
    - B. Many
    - C. Neither
    - D. None

15. There aren't any glasses on the shelf.

    There are _____ on the table, either.
    - A. some
    - B. a few
    - C. none
    - D. any

16. I think _____ took your umbrella.
    - A. anyone
    - B. one
    - C. person
    - D. someone

17. Sam has a lot of friends in Wickam City, but he doesn't know _____ in Colterville.
    - A. someone
    - B. anyone
    - C. any friend
    - D. any person

18. Maria isn't going _____ this weekend.
    - A. anywhere
    - B. to anywhere
    - C. somewhere
    - D. to somewhere

19. She doesn't know _____ about sports.
    - A. anything
    - B. something
    - C. nothing
    - D. none

20. I want to give my brother _____ for his birthday.
    A. a thing   C. anything
    B. something   D. any

21. His friend lives _____ on the other side of town.
    A. near   C. somewhere
    B. here   D. anywhere

22. Barbara doesn't have a car, _____ she takes the bus to work.
    A. as   C. then
    B. because   D. so

23. Jack's always reading books. He _____ like to read.
    A. will   C. would
    B. must   D. can

24. Sam worked hard today. He _____ be tired now.
    A. shall   C. will
    B. can   D. must

25. I hope everyone _____ to the party tomorrow.
    A. will come   C. come
    B. shall come   D. are coming

26. The phone is ringing. _____ I answer it?
    A. Will   C. Shall
    B. Would   D. Won't

27. You look hungry. _____ you like a sandwich?
    A. Will   C. Do
    B. Would   D. Can

28. She's asking _____ some questions.
    A. them   C. for them
    B. to them   D. of them

29. We bought a lamp for Mr. Poole. We gave it _____ last night.
    A. him   C. to her
    B. to him   D. for him

30. Albert likes Linda. He brought _____ some chocolates yesterday.
    A. for her   C. to her
    B. hers   D. her

31. They went _____ after school.
    A. to home   C. home
    B. at home   D. to the home

32. There are some good restaurants _____ Wickam City.
    A. at   C. in
    B. for   D. from

33. The boys are cleaning _____ shoes.
    A. there   C. theirs
    B. their   D. them

34. Is that umbrella _____?
    A. you   C. your
    B. to you   D. yours

35. Where are the glasses? _____ on the shelf.
    A. They're   C. Their
    B. There   D. There are

36. _____ bread in the kitchen.
    A. There are   C. It has
    B. There are some   D. There's some

37. She isn't _____ to lift that table.
    A. strong for   C. strong enough
    B. enough strong   D. very strong

38. He's _____ to work.
    A. too lazy   C. lazy enough
    B. very lazy   D. so lazy

39. We _____ dinner when the telephone rang.
    A. was having   C. have
    B. were having   D. are having

40. I _____ television when a bird flew into the room.
    A. was watching   C. looked at
    B. were watching   D. saw

41. Jimmy and Linda were walking home when

    they _____ a loud noise.
    A. saw   C. heard
    B. were hearing   D. met

42. Last year at this time Ula Hackey _____
    Hollywood.
    A. lived at   C. was living in
    B. was living at   D. is living in

43. Barbara and Tino _____ to the beach last
    Sunday.
    A. was   C. go
    B. went   D. were

44. Do they often go to the beach?

    Yes, they _____.
    A. do   C. do go
    B. go   D. are going

45. Does Albert have any new magazines?

    No, he _____
    A. does   C. has
    B. doesn't   D. don't

46. Nancy _____ to play tennis tomorrow.
    A. goes   C. will like
    B. is going   D. likes

47. Your friends aren't going to the post office,

    _____?
    A. do they   C. they are
    B. aren't they   D. are they

48. Linda was studying last night, _____?
    A. wasn't she   C. she was
    B. she wasn't   D. did she

49. Jimmy took a book from the shelf a few

    minutes ago. He's putting _____ now.
    A. it on   C. it back
    B. back it   D. them back

50. Gloria is a good dancer. She dances

    _____.
    A. good   C. very good
    B. goodly   D. well

CHAPTER NINE

Comparative

a

b

a Albert is twenty years old and Jimmy is seventeen. Albert is older than Jimmy. He's also heavier. He weighs 175 pounds. Jimmy only weighs 150 pounds. Jimmy is younger and thinner than Albert. And he's taller. Jimmy is five feet ten inches tall. Albert is only five feet seven inches tall.

1. Who's older, Albert or Jimmy?
2. Which one is heavier?
3. How much does Albert weigh?
4. How much does Jimmy weigh?
5. Is Albert taller than Jimmy?
6. How tall is Albert?
7. How tall is Jimmy?

b San Francisco and Los Angeles are both large cities. But Los Angeles is larger than San Francisco. It has a population of almost three million people. The population of San Francisco is less than one million. Los Angeles has very good weather. The weather in Los Angeles is better than in San Francisco. But the air in Los Angeles is bad. It's worse than in San Francisco.

1. Which of the two cities is larger?
2. What's the population of Los Angeles?
3. What's the population of San Francisco?
4. Which city has better weather?
5. Is the air better in Los Angeles than in San Francisco?

SHORT-WORD COMPARATIVE

Albert is older than Jimmy.
_____ bigger _____.
_____ heavier _____.
_____ shorter _____.

c *Complete the following sentences, using the comparative form.*

Examples: Jimmy is (tall) *taller* than Albert.

The air in Los Angeles is (bad) *worse* than in San Francisco.

1. Tino is (strong) _____ than Johnnie.

2. Mabel is (heavy) _____ than Linda.

3. A bicycle is (cheap) _____ than a motorcycle.

4. An airplane is (fast) _____ than a car.

5. Mr. Bascomb is (rich) _____ than Dr. Pasto.

6. Sam is (busy) _____ than Jack.

7. These glasses are (clean) _____ than those.

8. Your lessons are (easy) _____ than mine.

9. The weather in Los Angeles is (good) _____ than in San Francisco.

MABEL: Do you think Sunnyville is better than Fast City?

SAM: Sure. People are nicer in Sunnyville.

MABEL: But isn't it expensive there?

SAM: Sunnyville is cheaper than Fast City.

MABEL: What about the weather?

SAM: It's better in Sunnyville.

MABEL: Then why do some people prefer Fast City?

SAM: I don't know. I can't understand it.

SUNNYVILLE   population: 42,106   **FAST CITY**   population: 537,853

d *Ask and answer questions about the two cities. Use the comparative form.*

Example: friendly
Student A: **Which city is friendlier?**
Student B: **Sunnyville (is).**

1. clean   4. noisy   7. large
2. busy   5. safe   8. cheap
3. small   6. pretty   9. good

e *Make comparisons based on the information given.*

Examples: Jimmy weighs 150 pounds. Albert weighs 175 pounds.
           Jimmy is lighter than Albert.
           (Albert is heavier than Jimmy.)

           Los Angeles doesn't get much rain. It rains a lot in San Francisco.
           Los Angeles is drier than San Francisco.
           (San Francisco is wetter than Los Angeles.)

1. Johnnie can lift 100 pounds. Tino can lift 300 pounds.
2. Mr. Bascomb has a lot of money. Sam doesn't have very much.
3. Peter is five feet ten inches tall. Tino is six feet tall.
4. Peter's car is five years old. Tino's car is eight years old.
5. Peter's car can go 120 miles per hour. Tino's car can go 90 miles per hour.
6. Mrs. Golo weighs 125 pounds. Mrs. Brown weighs 155 pounds.
7. Johnnie takes a shower twice a day. Barney takes a shower twice a week.
8. Barbara is twenty-four years old. Tino is twenty-nine years old.
9. Wickam City is an average-sized town. Colterville is very small.

a

Rolls Royce   Volkswagen

b

Nancy   Maria

Maria

Nancy

Nancy

a The Rolls Royce is a very expensive car. It's much more expensive than a Volkswagen. It's also more elegant and more comfortable. And of course, a Rolls Royce is more powerful than a Volkswagen. However, the Volkswagen is a very popular car. It's more practical than a Rolls Royce. That's because it's smaller and more economical. It can travel twenty-five miles on a gallon of gas.

1. Which car is more expensive?
2. Which car is more elegant?
3. Is a Volkswagen more comfortable than a Rolls Royce?
4. Which car is more powerful?
5. Which car is more practical?
6. Is a Volkswagen more economical than a Rolls Royce?
7. How many miles can a Volkswagen travel on a gallon of gas?

b Nancy and Maria are both attractive women. But Maria is more attractive than Nancy. She is also more artistic. She likes to paint and draw. On the other hand, Nancy is more adventurous. She flies an airplane and rides a motorcycle. She is also more athletic. She likes to play all kinds of sports.

1. Which of the two women is more attractive?
2. Which of them is more artistic?
3. What does Maria like to do?
4. Is she more adventurous than Nancy?
5. Which woman is more athletic?
6. What does Nancy like to do?

LONG-WORD COMPARATIVE

Maria is more attractive than Nancy.
_____ artistic _____.
_____ elegant _____.
_____ popular _____.

c *Complete the following sentences, as indicated.*

Examples: Nancy is attractive, but Maria *is more attractive*.

   Los Angeles is a beautiful city, but San Francisco *is more beautiful*.

1. Linda is athletic, but Jimmy _____.

2. Basketball is a popular sport, but football _____.

3. A Cadillac is expensive, but a Rolls Royce _____.

4. A Volkswagen is economical, but a bicycle _____.

5. Barney is interesting, but Dr. Pasto _____.

6. Maria is energetic, but Nancy _____.

7. Mr. Bascomb is intelligent, but Dr. Pasto _____.

8. French is a difficult language, but German _____.

BARNEY: You know Sam Brown and Mr. Bascomb, don't you? They're good friends of yours, aren't they?

JACK: That's right. All of us belong to the Lions Club.

BARNEY: Do you think Mr. Bascomb is more successful than Sam?

JACK: That's a difficult question. Both men are good at their jobs.

BARNEY: Well, which one is more industrious?

JACK: I don't know. They both work very hard.

BARNEY: Do you think Sam is more popular than Mr. Bascomb?

JACK: Sure. Sam has more friends than anyone else in town.

BARNEY: But Mr. Bascomb is more generous than Sam, isn't he?

JACK: Only with his money.

BARNEY: You mean Sam is more generous with his time?

JACK: That's right. Last year he worked as a volunteer for the Fire Department.

BARNEY: That's interesting. Well, thanks for the information.

JACK: Wait a minute. Why are you asking all these questions?

BARNEY: So we can make a decision. We're trying to decide who will be the next Man of the Year.

d   *Ask and answer questions about these two men. Use the comparative form.*

Example: industrious
Student A: **Who's more industrious, Sam or Mr. Bascomb?**
Student B: **Mr. Bascomb is.**
Student C: **You're right.**   OR   **You're wrong. Sam's more industrious.**

1. pleasant   4. energetic   7. sociable
2. successful   5. relaxed   8. intelligent
3. popular   6. ambitious   9. polite

e   *Complete the following sentences, using* **more than** *or* **less than,** *whichever seems more appropriate.*

Examples: Jimmy is (energetic) ___*more energetic*___ than Albert.

Fred is (intelligent) ___*less intelligent*___ than Dr. Pasto.

1. A bicycle is (expensive) _____ than a car.

2. A Volkswagen is (economical) _____ than a Rolls Royce.

3. It's (powerful) _____ than a Rolls Royce.

4. Sam is (popular) _____ than anyone else in town.

5. He's (industrious) _____ than his friends.

6. Maria is (athletic) _____ than Nancy.

7. Life in the country is (peaceful) _____ than in the city.

8. Brasília is (modern) _____ than the average city.

9. Nancy Paine is (famous) _____ than Sophia Loren.

Last Saturday the Browns drove out to see the farm. Mr. Fix was standing in front of the farmhouse when they arrived.

"This is the place," he said. "You're really in the country now." He smiled as the Browns got out of their car and walked over to him. Mabel spoke first. "It's a long way from the city," she said. "It's farther than I thought."

"It's more peaceful that way," said Mr. Fix. "Just smell the air. It's cleaner here than in the city. And the farmhouse is very attractive, don't you think?"

"It's older and smaller than in the pictures," said Mabel. "And the barn doesn't look very solid."

"The house needs a paint job," said Sam. "And the gate is broken."

"You can fix it, Sam. That will be good exercise for you," said Mr. Fix.

"You said there was a stream, Mr. Fix. Where is it?"

"Well, this is the dry season," he explained. "It isn't very big this time of year."

"I can't even see it," said Jimmy. "And those fruit trees don't look very healthy."

"They just need a little water," said Mr. Fix.

"That horse is in pretty bad shape," said Sam. "He looked better in the picture."

"He just needs a little exercise," said Mr. Fix.

"I'm sorry Mr. Fix," said Sam. "This farm is much worse than I expected. I was hoping for something better and less expensive."

"Okay," said Mr. Fix, throwing his hands up in the air. "I give up." He was in a bad mood and left in a hurry. But when he got in the car and turned the key, nothing happened. "Oh no," he said. "I didn't get enough gas. The tank is empty."

Sam looked at him severely. "You can start walking, Mr. Fix."

"Why do you say that, Sam?"

"Because we're a long way from town and it's later than you think. Besides," he said, smiling, "it will be good exercise for you."

a *Answer the following questions about the story.*

1. Where did the Browns go last Saturday?
2. Who was standing in front of the farmhouse when they arrived?
3. Did the house look the same as in the pictures?
4. What did the house need?
5. What was wrong with the gate?
6. What was wrong with the horse?
7. Did Sam decide to take the farm?
8. What was he hoping for?
9. Why didn't Mr. Fix's car start when he turned the key?
10. Did Sam offer to help Mr. Fix?

b *Complete the following sentences, as indicated.*

Examples: That radio isn't very good. This one is much *better*.

Their apartment isn't very comfortable. Ours is a lot *more comfortable*.

Jack isn't very industrious. Fred is even *less industrious*.

1. Johnnie isn't very strong. Tino is a lot _____.

2. My brother isn't very energetic. My sister is even _____.

3. Mr. Bascomb is generous, but Sam is even _____.

4. Your dictionary is good. But I think mine is a little _____.

5. Their car isn't very economical. Ours is a lot _____.

6. Dr. Pasto is busy, but Mr. Bascomb is even _____.

7. Mr. Golo is a bad dancer, but his wife is even _____.

8. Maria isn't very adventurous. Nancy is a lot _____.

9. Fred doesn't think politics is very interesting. He thinks football is even

_____.

Jack's car
price: $5,000
mileage: 19 miles per gallon
maximum speed: 90 miles per hour

Mr. Bascomb's car
price: $19,000
mileage: 14 miles per gallon
maximum speed: 120 miles
per hour

c   *Make sentences comparing Jack's car with Mr. Bascomb's car.*

1. long / short   *Jack's car is shorter than Mr. Bascomb's.*
                   Mr. Bascomb's car is longer than Jack's.

2. big / small   _____

                   _____

3. fast / slow   _____

                   _____

4. light / heavy   _____

                   _____

5. clean / dirty   _____

                   _____

6. old / new   _____

                   _____

1. economical   **Jack's car is <u>more economical</u> than Mr. Bascomb's.**
                   Mr. Bascomb's car is <u>less economical</u> than Jack's.

2. powerful
3. expensive
4. practical
5. comfortable
6. elegant

d   *Answer the following questions as indicated.*

Examples: Sam is more popular than Mr. Bascomb, isn't he?
Yes, he is.

Linda is older than Nancy, isn't she?
No, she isn't. Nancy is older than Linda.

1. Sam is taller than Mabel, isn't he?
2. Jimmy is heavier than Albert, isn't he?
3. Barbara and Tino are younger than Sam and Mabel, aren't they?
4. Jack is richer than Mr. Bascomb, isn't he?
5. Barbara is more attractive than Anne, isn't she?
6. Fred is more intelligent than Dr. Pasto, isn't he?
7. Sunnyville is cheaper than Fast City, isn't it?
8. San Francisco is bigger than Los Angeles, isn't it?
9. The weather in Hawaii is warmer than the weather in Alaska, isn't it?
10. A Volkswagen is faster than a Porsche, isn't it?
11. A bicycle is more economical than a car, isn't it?
12. Barney is more famous than Muhammad Ali, isn't he?

e   *Complete the following sentences using the conjunctions so, when, while, because, however, and although.*

Examples: She was looking out the window ___*when*___ she heard a loud noise.

They were watching television *while* ___ I was having dinner.

1. _____ she's very attractive, she doesn't have many friends.

2. He doesn't like rock music, _____ he never goes to discotheques.

3. _____ the weather is good, everyone goes to the beach.

4. She didn't finish the housework _____ she had lots of time.

5. He was listening to the radio _____ she was reading the newspaper.

6. They're having a lot of problems. _____, they try not to worry.

7. You always know _____ Mr. Fix is in a bad mood.

8. He was in a hurry this morning, _____ he didn't have breakfast.

9. It's a beautiful day for the beach. _____, we plan to stay home and study.

10. People like Sam _____ he's friendly.

11. Jimmy is a good basketball player _____ he isn't very tall.

12. I don't enjoy sports very much. _____, I do like basketball.

ONE STEP FURTHER

The Brown family had an unpleasant experience with Mr. Fix.
1. What's your opinion of Mr. Fix?
2. What did he say or imply about the farm that wasn't true?
3. Why did Sam refuse to give Mr. Fix a ride into town?
4. Do you think Sam did the right thing? Why or why not?
5. Did you ever have an experience with a dishonest salesman? If so, what were the circumstances?

Everyone admires Mr. Brown. He's an outstanding citizen.
1. Who do you admire?
2. What are his or her outstanding qualities?
3. Why do you consider these qualities important?

SKETCH

Select one student to be Barney. Select another student to be Nancy.
Situation: Barney invites Nancy to have lunch with him at Joe's Cafe. Nancy declines the invitation and gives an excuse for not going. Barney asks if she would like to meet for lunch another day.

Select one student to play Mr. Fix. Select two other students to play Sam and Mabel.
Situation: Have the students re-enact the story on pages 153 and 154 while adding their own ideas.

CONVERSATION PRACTICE

1. Pairs of students discuss their ideal choice for "Man of the Year" or "Woman of the Year." Each student tries to convince the other that his or her choice is better.
2. Pairs of students discuss their favorite cities. Each student argues that his or her choice is better.

COMPOSITION

1. Describe an experience you had with a dishonest salesman. What did you learn from that experience?
2. Who is your choice for "Man of the Year" or "Woman of the Year"? Give reasons for your selection.
3. Compare two friends, two members of your family, or two famous people.
4. Compare two cities or two countries.
5. Describe the people in your home town or in the town you're living in now. How are they different from people in other parts of the country?

VOCABULARY

adventurous	decision	gate	mileage	severely
age (n.)		generous	million	solid
artistic	economical		mood	speed (n.)
athletic	elegant	hand (n.)		stream (n.)
attractive	exercise (n.)	healthy	nothing	successful
average (adj.)	explain	horse		
			offer (v.)	twice
barn	farmhouse	inch (n.)		
break (v.)	fast (adj.)	industrious	population	volunteer (n.)
	foot (n.)		pound (n.)	
choice (n.)		light (adj.)	powerful	weigh
comfortable	gallon		practical	winner
		maximum		

EXPRESSIONS

They're good at their jobs.   I give up.   It's a long way from town.
It's in pretty bad shape.   He was in a bad mood.   It's later than you think.

PRONUNCIATION

m	**n**	
come	ten	dinner
home	pen	winner
same	thin	thinner
time	begin	beginner

The game will begin at ten past nine.
The thin swimmer is the winner.
Take him some ham for dinner.

	ng	
long	bring	singer
song	young	singing
ring	wedding	ringing
thing	building	bringing

The young couple is buying a wedding ring.
He's bringing his painting this evening.
She's making something interesting.

Slim is buying a young chicken for dinner.
The phone is ringing in the living room.
Sam sang the same song nine times.

SHORT-WORD COMPARATIVE

He's	older stronger	than his friend.

He's	bigger fatter	than his friend.

She's	prettier friendlier	than her sister.

Irregular

You have a	good typewriter. bad dictionary.

It's	better worse	than mine.

LONG-WORD COMPARATIVE

Their car is	more	expensive powerful	than ours.
	less	economical practical	

CHAPTER TEN

**Present perfect:
regular and
irregular verbs**

**Present perfect
with ''for''
and ''since''**

**Present perfect/
past simple
contrast**

DR. PASTO'S LIFE

Dr. Pasto has had a very interesting life. He has traveled around the world. He has visited the Great Wall of China. He has lived in Egypt and India. He has worked as a cook, lifeguard, photographer, and teacher.

PRESENT PERFECT: REGULAR VERBS

Barney's visited the Art Museum.	They've attended several lectures on art.
He's _____.	You've _____.
Nancy's _____.	We've_____.
She's _____.	I've_____.

a   *Complete the following sentences, using the present perfect.*

Examples: Barney (invite) Nancy to a lecture.
            Barney's invited Nancy to a lecture.

            They (attend) several lectures this year.
            They've attended several lectures this year.

1. Maria (paint) some beautiful pictures.
2. Sam (work) very hard.
3. Linda (clean) the kitchen.
4. Jimmy (wash) the dishes.
5. They (finish) all the housework.
6. They (decide) to see a movie.
7. They (look at) the cinema guide.
8. They (call) Albert.
9. They (invite) him to the movie.

NEGATIVE

Barney hasn't visited the Music Center.	They haven't attended any concerts.
He_____.	You _____.
Nancy _____.	We _____.
She _____.	I _____.

b   *Make negative sentences using the present perfect.*

Examples: Dr. Pasto has lived in India.   (in Pakistan)
            But he hasn't lived in Pakistan.

            Sam and Jimmy have fished in the mountains.   (in the ocean)
            But they haven't fished in the ocean.

1. Jimmy's washed the dishes.   (the pots and pans)
2. Linda's cleaned the kitchen.   (the living room)
3. They've helped their mother.   (their father)
4. Sam and Mabel have painted the bedroom.   (the bathroom)
5. They've finished the housework.   (the yardwork)
6. Barney's repaired his car.   (his radio)
7. Anne's learned to play the guitar.   (the piano)
8. Mr. and Mrs. Golo have traveled in Mexico.   (in Central America)
9. They've stayed in Mexico City.   (in Tampico)

It's nine o'clock Monday morning.

So far, Mrs. Golo
has taken a shower . . .

. . . gotten dressed

. . . eaten breakfast

. . . read the newspaper

and fed the cat.

Right now she's walking to
the bus stop. She's going
to work.

PRESENT PERFECT: IRREGULAR VERBS

Mrs. Golo's eaten breakfast.   They've fed the cat.
She's _____.   You've _____.
Mr. Golo's_____.   We've _____.
He's _____.   I've _____.

c *Make sentences using the present perfect.*

Examples: Mrs. Golo's eaten breakfast.   (We)
           We've eaten breakfast, too.

           Anne and Barbara have gone to work.   (Tino)
           Tino's gone to work, too.

1. Peter and Maria have been to Europe.   (Nancy)
2. They've met a lot of interesting people.   (She)
3. Dr. Pasto's had an interesting life.   (I)
4. He's had some good times.   (We)
5. Mr. Bascomb has made a lot of money.   (Our friends)
6. He's given a lot to charity.   (They)
7. Maria's had some good parties.   (You)
8. Jimmy and Linda have gone to the market.   (Albert)
9. Barney's eaten at the Martinoli Restaurant.   (We)

NEGATIVE

Mrs. Golo hasn't eaten lunch.   They haven't fed the dog.
She _____.   You _____.
Mr. Golo _____.   We_____.
He_____.   I _____.

d *Make sentences in the negative, using the present perfect.*

Examples: Anne has met Tino.   (Johnnie)
           But she hasn't met Johnnie.

           Mr. and Mrs. Bascomb have had Italian food.   (Mexican food)
           But they haven't had Mexican food.

1. Mr. Bascomb has given money to the City Hospital.   (the Public Library)
2. He's paid the gas bill.   (the water bill)
3. The Hambys have been to France.   (to England)
4. They've seen the Eiffel Tower.   (the Tower of London)
5. They've heard the Paris Symphony Orchestra.   (the London Symphony Orchestra)
6. Dr. Pasto's written short stories.   (poetry)
7. Barney's driven a bus.   (a truck)
8. I've spoken to Sam.   (Mabel)
9. We've bought a new refrigerator.   (a new stove)

DR. PASTO: Have you seen any movies this week?

MARIA: No, but I saw a good one last week.

DR. PASTO: What was the name of it?

MARIA: *An American in Paris* with Gene
               Kelly.

DR. PASTO: I know the one. I've seen it three
               times.

MARIA: Wasn't it a wonderful picture? I
               liked it because the story took
               place in Paris.

DR. PASTO: Have you ever been to Paris?

MARIA: Yes. I studied medicine at the
               University of Paris. Didn't you
               know?

e *Answer the questions about the pictures, as indicated.*

1. A: **Has Maria been to Paris?**
    B: **Yes, she has.**

2. A: **Have the Hambys paid their electric bill?**
    B: **No, they haven't.**

3. Have Sam and Mabel been to the market?

4. Has Mrs. Golo fed the cat?

5. Has Marty caught any fish?

6. Have Fred and Barney caught any fish?

7. Have Ed and Brutus eaten dinner?

8. Has Ed shaved recently?

a

b

a Mr. Bascomb has worked at the City Bank for twenty years. He has been president for five years. The City Bank has changed a lot since he became president. In the past, it was just an average bank. But now it's the number one bank in Wickam City. Mr. Bascomb has always worked very hard. He hasn't taken a vacation since 1975.

1. How long has Mr. Bascomb worked at the City Bank?
2. How long has he been president?
3. How has the City Bank changed since Mr. Bascomb became president?
4. Has Mr. Bascomb taken any vacations recently?

b Barbara and Tino have gone out together for three years. Their relationship became serious a few months ago, and they decided to get married. Barbara and Tino have been engaged since last July. They are going to get married in a couple of weeks. Today they are looking for a wedding ring.

1. How long have Barbara and Tino gone out together?
2. When did they decide to get married?
3. How long have they been engaged?
4. When are they going to get married?
5. What are they doing today?

PRESENT PERFECT WITH FOR

They've gone out together for three years.
_____ a few months.
_____ several weeks.
_____ a long time.

c *Answer the following questions using the present perfect with **for**.*

Examples: How long has Mr. Bascomb worked at the City Bank?   (twenty years)
He's worked at the City Bank for twenty years.

How long have Barbara and Tino been engaged?   (several weeks)
They've been engaged for several weeks.

1. How long have the Browns been in Wickam City?   (a long time)
2. How long have they lived in the same house?   (many years)
3. How long has Linda studied French?   (several months)
4. How long has Jimmy played football?   (a few years)
5. How long have they known Albert?   (a long time)
6. How long has Albert driven a car?   (one year)
7. How long has he had his new typewriter?   (several weeks)
8. How long has Barbara worked at the City Bank?   (a couple of years)
9. How long has Otis been a painter?   (ten years)

JIMMY BROWN: How long have you known
                  Mr. Grubb?

SAM BROWN: I've known him for thirty
                  years.

JIMMY BROWN: Then you've been friends
                  since high school.

SAM BROWN: That's right, Jimmy.

LINDA BROWN: Has Dad always worn the
                  same hat?

MABEL BROWN: Yes. He's had it since our
                  marriage.

LINDA BROWN: Why doesn't he buy a
                  new hat?

MABEL BROWN: He can't find a good one.

LINDA BROWN: How long has he looked?

MABEL BROWN: He's looked for months.
                  It's hopeless.

PRESENT PERFECT WITH <u>SINCE</u>

They've been friends since high school.
_____ 1958.
_____ they were sixteen.

d   *Answer the following questions using the present perfect with* **since.**

Examples: How long has Sam worn the same hat?   (his marriage)
He's worn the same hat <u>since</u> his marriage.

How long have Sam and Jack been friends?   (high school)
They've been friends <u>since</u> high school.

1. How long have Sam and Jack lived in Wickam City?   (their childhood)
2. How long have they belonged to the Lions Club?   (1978)
3. How long have the Browns had a garden?   (last spring)
4. How long has Linda studied music?   (high school)
5. How long has Otis painted pictures?   (he was a little boy)
6. How long has Jimmy known Albert?   (1982)
7. How long has Albert driven a car?   (last year)
8. How long have Barbara and Tino been engaged?   (last July)
9. How long have they played tennis together?   (last year)

PRESENT PERFECT WITH <u>FOR</u>

Sam's looked for a new hat for months.
_____ several weeks.
_____ a long time.

PRESENT PERFECT WITH <u>SINCE</u>

He's looked since April.
_____ last spring.
_____ his birthday.

e   *Answer the following questions using the present perfect with* **for or since.**

Examples: How long has Barbara worked at the bank?   (a couple of years)
She's worked at the bank <u>for</u> a couple of years.

How long has Anne worked at the bank?   (last year)
She's worked at the bank <u>since</u> last year.

1. How long has Albert had his new typewriter?   (last month)
2. How long has Maria been a doctor?   (a few years)
3. How long has Mr. Bascomb worked at the bank?   (twenty years)
4. How long have the Golos lived in Wickam City?   (several years)
5. How long have they enjoyed classical music?   (they were teenagers)
6. How long has Johnnie owned the book shop?   (a couple of years)
7. How long has he worn glasses?   (he was a little boy)
8. How long have your friends been in town?   (last month)
9. How long have they stayed at the same hotel?   (three weeks)

Elmer Coggins has been a farmer all his life. He has raised pigs and chickens for twenty years. He has grown a lot of corn, and his pigs have always been fat and healthy. However, this has been a bad year for Elmer. The weather has been dry for several weeks. It hasn't rained since March, and now it's June. Elmer is worried about his corn. Insects have destroyed part of his crop. Elmer hopes it will rain soon, so he won't lose the entire crop. He is also worried about his animals. His pigs are suffering and have lost a lot of weight. Elmer can't feed them well because he has very little corn. His chickens have done badly, too. They have laid very few eggs recently. The situation hasn't been this bad since 1978. That was the year Elmer's house burned down.

a   *Answer the following questions about the story.*

1. How long has Elmer been a farmer?
2. How long has he raised pigs and chickens?
3. What kind of year has this been for Elmer?
4. How long has the weather been dry?
5. When was the last time it rained?
6. Why is Elmer worried about his corn?
7. Why does Elmer hope it will rain?
8. What's happened to his pigs?
9. Why can't he feed them well?
10. How have Elmer's chickens done?
11. Has the situation always been this bad?
12. What happened in 1978?

b   *Complete the following sentences using the present perfect with **since**.*

Examples: Otis and Gloria visited the museum last month, **but they haven't visited the museum since.**

Fred called last night, **but he hasn't called since.**

1. Our friends were here last month, . . .
2. I spoke to them a few weeks ago, . . .
3. Jimmy and Linda watched television last weekend, . . .
4. Linda forgot her books two weeks ago, . . .
5. They saw Albert last Sunday, . . .
6. It rained a couple of days ago, . . .
7. We traveled last year, . . .
8. Fred worked in 1980, . . .
9. He voted a few years ago, . . .

c   *Make questions with **who, what,** or **where**.*

Examples: Mr. and Mrs. Golo have gone to the market.
Where have they gone?

Dr. Pasto has met the President.
Who has he met?

Linda has done her homework.
What has she done?

1. Maria has studied in Paris.
2. She's spoken to Dr. Pasto.
3. They've seen the same movie.
4. Albert has called Linda.
5. They've decided to go to the park.
6. Albert has put on a clean shirt.
7. Sam has written to his brother.
8. He's gone to the post office.
9. He's taken his umbrella.

d   *Ask and answer questions using the present perfect.*

Example: cat Japanese food
Student A: **Have you ever eaten Japanese food?**
Student B: **Yes, I have. I ate in a Japanese restaurant last month.**
             OR   No, I haven't. But I've eaten Chinese food.

1. lose your keys
2. repair anything
3. visit a factory
4. go to the mountains
5. fish in the ocean
6. eat a hamburger
7. wear a cowboy hat
8. meet a famous person
9. see a play
10. write a poem
11. make a long distance call
12. travel outside of the country

e   *Make negative questions as indicated.*

Examples: Did you hear that story?   Was it interesting?
            Didn't you hear that story?   **Wasn't it interesting?**

1. Are they going to the beach?
2. Did she come to the party?
3. Do you have a pen?
4. Have you read that book?
5. Were they having dinner?
6. Has he called you?
7. Is he arriving tomorrow?
8. Can he come later?
9. Are there any apples left?
10. Will you make some coffee?

f   *Complete the following sentences using appropriate nouns. There can be more than one appropriate noun for each sentence.*

Example: I'm going to the ___*market*___ to buy some milk.

1. The _____ is usually hot and dry at this time of year.

2. The people on our street are very friendly. We like all of our _____.

3. The _____ for this apartment is three hundred dollars a month.

4. All the _____ in the living room is new except for the sofa.

5. I work very hard. I haven't taken a _____ since 1980.

6. I live a long _____ from my job.

7. My office is in a large _____ on State Street.

8. Joe's Cafe is usually empty. He doesn't have many _____.

9. People don't like to eat at Joe's because the _____ is terrible.

10. This morning Joe had an _____ and broke some plates.

11. Peter usually has cereal for _____ in the morning.

12. He brushes his teeth after every _____.

LUNCH TIME

g   *Look at the picture and talk about what the people are doing. Then answer the following questions.*

1. Have you ever eaten at a sidewalk cafe? Are sidewalk cafes popular in your country?
2. What's the difference between a cafeteria and a restaurant? Do you pay tips in a cafeteria?
3. When was the last time you had a picnic? Where was it?
4. What kind of things can you cook on a barbecue?
5. What kind of food can you buy from a catering truck?
6. Do you sometimes take your lunch to work or school?
7. Do you like to cook? What kind of dishes can you make?
8. What are the advantages of eating at home? Eating out?
9. What do you think of American food? What is typical American food? Do you think Americans eat well?
10. Talk about the food in your country. What are some typical dishes? What kind of food do you like best?

ONE STEP FURTHER

Peter loves to travel. He wants to visit every part of the world.
1. Do you like to travel? Why or why not?
2. What are some of the countries that you would like to visit? Why do you want to visit these places?
3. What places do tourists like to visit in your country? Why are these places popular?
4. Do you think tourism is a good thing? Why or why not?

SKETCH

Select one student to be a tourist representative for his country. Select another student to be a traveler who wants to visit that country.
Situation: the tourist representative answers the traveler's questions about his country, including interesting places to visit, the weather, transportation, food, hotels, shopping, etc.

COMPOSITION

1. Write about an interesting place you have visited.
2. Write about tourism in your country. Describe the main tourist attractions, the weather, transportation, shopping, entertainment, etc.
3. Describe an interesting book you have read.
4. Describe an interesting movie or play you have seen this year.
5. Compare American food with the food in your country.

VOCABULARY

become	engaged	lay (v.)	serious
burn (v.)	engagement	lifeguard	since (adv.)
			since. (conj.)
change (v.)	farmer	marriage	since (prep.)
childhood			suffer
crop (n.)	glasses	part	
	grow	past (n.)	yardwork
destroy		pig	
	high school		
economics	hopeless	raise	
		recently	
	insect	relationship	
		ring (n.)	

EXPRESSIONS

It's hopeless.   It's the number one bank in town.
Didn't you know?   The story took place in Paris.

PRONUNCIATION

	l	
like	dollar	family
look	belong	hotel
love	college	small
leave	help	pull

The tall policeman seldom smiled.
He left a small yellow envelope by the telephone.
Sally lived alone in a small hotel.

	r	
rest	order	work
radio	corner	care
ripe	camera	her
repeat	very	your

He drove a red truck to work every day.
Where was your sister yesterday morning?
We never drink water in the afternoon.

The yellow roses are lovely.
Your girlfriend always arrives late to work.
She wrote a long letter to her brother last Friday.

PRESENT PERFECT   Affirmative

He She	's (has)	taken a shower. had breakfast.
I You We They	've (have)	washed the dishes. cleaned the kitchen.

Negative

He She	hasn't (has not)	taken a shower. had breakfast.
I You We They	haven't (have not)	washed the dishes. cleaned the kitchen.

Interrogative

Has	he she	taken a shower? had breakfast?
Have	I you we they	washed the dishes? cleaned the kitchen?

Short Answers

Yes,	he she	has.
	I you we they	have.

No,	he she	hasn't.
	I you we they	haven't.

Regular Verbs

He's (He has)	washed cleaned repaired painted	the car.

Irregular Verbs

She's (She has)	lost found taken forgotten	the money.

PRESENT PERFECT with FOR and SINCE

| They've
(They have) | worked
lived | in Wickam City | for several weeks.
a few months.
a long time. |
			January. since last year. 1975.

Negative

| We haven't
(We have not) | seen
spoken to | Mr. Poole | for a few weeks.
a couple of months.
a long time. |
			last month. since August. summer vacation.

CHAPTER ELEVEN

**Infinitive
of purpose
Present perfect
with ''just''**

**Present perfect
with ''already''
and ''yet''**

a

b

a The Browns receive their mail every day at eleven o'clock. It's five minutes past eleven. The postman has just delivered some letters. Mabel is going outside to get the mail. She is expecting a letter from her sister in Los Angeles.

1. When do the Browns receive their mail?
2. What time is it now?
3. What has the postman just done?
4. Why is Mabel going outside?
5. What is she expecting?

b Anne Jones and Johnnie Wilson both live in the same neighborhood. They have some friends in common, but they have never met each other before. Anne has just entered Johnnie's Bookshop for the first time. She wants to buy a Chinese cookbook. Johnnie has just seen her. He thinks she is very attractive.

1. What do Anne and Johnnie have in common?
2. Have they met each other before?
3. Has Anne been to Johnnie's Bookshop before?
4. What does she want to buy?
5. Has Johnnie seen Anne before?
6. What's his impression of her?

INFINITIVE OF PURPOSE

She's going outside to get the mail.
_____ to talk with the postman.
_____ to feed the dog.
_____ to work in the garden.

c *Combine the following sentences, as indicated.*

Examples: Mabel is going outside. She's going to get the mail.
She's going outside to get the mail.

Anne has gone to the bookshop. She wants to buy a cookbook.
She's gone to the bookshop to buy a cookbook.

1. Albert and Linda are going to the library. They're going to study.
2. Mrs. Golo has gone to the market. She wants to buy some vegetables.
3. We're going to the airport. We're going to meet a friend.
4. Peter is going to the University. He's going to attend a lecture.
5. Sam and Mabel have gone to the post office. They want to buy some stamps.
6. Nancy is going home. She's going to make dinner.
7. Fred has gone to the bank. He wants to borrow some money.
8. Jack is saving his money. He wants to buy a new car.
9. The boys have gone to the park. They're going to play football.

PRESENT PERFECT WITH <u>JUST</u>

Peter's just arrived.	They've just received some letters.
He's_____.	You've_____.
Nancy's_____.	We've _____.
She's _____.	I've _____.

d *Make sentences using the present perfect with **just**.*

Examples: Anne and Johnnie met each other a short time ago.

They've just met each other.

Mabel turned off the light a few seconds ago.

She's just turned off the light.

1. Mr. Bascomb recovered from his illness yesterday.

_____

2. He received a telegram a little while ago.

_____

3. Anne called the hospital a couple of minutes ago.

_____

4. She spoke to the doctor a few seconds ago.

_____

5. Our friends arrived in town this morning.

_____

6. They moved into a hotel an hour ago.

_____

7. They called us a few minutes ago.

_____

8. We had breakfast a very short time ago.

_____

9. I washed the dishes a couple of minutes ago.

_____

a

b

a Barbara is getting ready to go out. She has a date with Tino tonight. She has already taken a bath and gotten dressed. Right now she is brushing her hair. Barbara hasn't put on her makeup yet. She is going to do that next.

1. Why is Barbara getting ready to go out?
2. Is she going to take a bath?
3. Has she already gotten dressed?
4. What's she doing now?
5. Has she put on her makeup yet?

b Peter loves to travel and he has a great ambition: he wants to visit every part of the world. He has already been to Europe, Asia, and South America. But he hasn't been to Africa yet. He plans to go there next. He thinks it will be a great adventure.

1. What does Peter love to do?
2. What is his great ambition?
3. Has he already been to Europe?
4. Has he gone to Africa yet?
5. Does he plan to go there next?
6. What does he think a trip to Africa will be like?

AFFIRMATIVE

Peter's already been to Europe.
He's_____.
Maria's _____.
She's _____.

They've already visited France.
You've _____.
We've _____.
I've _____.

c *Answer the following questions using the present perfect with* **already***.*

Examples: Is Barbara going to take a bath?
No, she's already taken a bath.

Are Mr. and Mrs. Bascomb going to read the newspaper?
No, they've already read the newspaper.

1. Are Jimmy and Linda going to have dinner?
2. Are they going to do their homework?
3. Are we going to study Chapter Ten?
4. Is Barney going to fix up his taxi?
5. Is he going to pay back Mr. Bascomb?
6. Is Mrs. Golo going to feed the cat?
7. Are the Browns going to paint their house?
8. Are they going to plant some tomatoes?
9. Is Anne going to clean the windows?

BARBARA: Hello Anne. How's everything?

ANNE: Fine. I met a nice boy last week.

BARBARA: Have you gone out with him yet?

ANNE: Not yet. But he's already called me three times.

BARBARA: When will you see him again?

ANNE: Tomorrow. We're going to have dinner together.

SAM BROWN: What would you like to do today?

MABEL BROWN: I'd like to go to the Art Museum.

SAM BROWN: Are you serious? We've already been there twice this month.

MABEL BROWN: But we haven't seen their new exhibition yet.

SAM BROWN: What exhibition?

MABEL BROWN: The one that started last Monday.

d   *Ask and answer questions about the pictures, as indicated.*

1. ☑ take out trash   ☐ sweep sidewalk

A. **Has Fred taken out the trash and swept the sidewalk?**
B: **He's taken out the trash, but he hasn't swept the sidewalk yet.**

2. ☑ clean kitchen   ☐ living room

A: **Have Jimmy and Linda cleaned the kitchen and the living room?**
B: **They've cleaned the kitchen, but they haven't cleaned the living room yet.**

3. ☑ repair roof   ☐ door

4. ☑ feed dog   ☐ cat

5. ☑ paint bedroom   ☐ bathroom

6. ☑ wash car   ☐ cut grass

7. ☑ wash dishes   ☐ take out trash

8. ☑ clean windows   ☐ make bed

Last night Anne and Johnnie had their first date. Johnnie wanted to do
something special, so he invited Anne to have dinner at Captain Morgan's,
a new restaurant named after the famous English pirate.

"Have you been here before?" asked Anne, as they entered the restaurant.

"No," said Johnnie. "But I hear it's very good. The seafood is supposed
to be out of this world."

"Welcome to Captain Morgan's," said a young woman wearing an
exotic red dress. "I'm your hostess."

"Good evening," said Johnnie. "We'd like a table for two."

"Do you have reservations?"

"No, we don't," said Johnnie. "I didn't think it was necessary."

"It's all right—I'll find you a table. This way, please."

Anne and Johnnie followed the hostess to the back of the restaurant.
"Here we are," she said, motioning to a small table in the corner.

"It's too noisy here," said Johnnie. "I can hear plates in the kitchen."

"Can't you give us another table?" asked Anne.

"I'm sorry. This is the only table that's free."

"Then we'll wait for another one," said Johnnie.

"OK," said the hostess, "but you'll have to wait at least an hour. There
are several people ahead of you with reservations."

Johnnie was very disappointed. He turned to Anne. "What do you
think?" he asked.

"This table is OK," said Anne. "We can sit here."

The hostess smiled. "I'll get the waiter," she said.

Anne and Johnnie were looking at the menu when they heard a deep voice.

"Good evening," said a big man dressed like a pirate. "I'm Blackbeard, your waiter."

"Good evening," said Johnnie.

"Have you decided yet?" asked Blackbeard.

"No, we don't understand the menu. Everything's in French."

"Of course," said Blackbeard. "French is the language of food."

"What do you recommend, Mr. Blackbeard?" asked Anne.

"The specialty of the house. Poisson cru à la mode."

"What's that?"

"Raw fish. You'll love it."

"OK," said Johnnie. "Bring us two of those and a bottle of white wine."

"Very good," said Blackbeard.

"Here's your dinner," said Blackbeard, setting two plates of fish on the table. "Bon appetit."

"Thank you," said Johnnie.

"Don't these fish look fresh?" said Anne, picking up her knife and fork.

"Yes, they look . . . alive!" said Johnnie. "My fish is moving!"

"So is mine," said Anne. "It's jumping on the plate."

"Waiter!" said Johnnie. "These fish are still alive. You served us live fish!"

"Of course," said Blackbeard calmly. "That's poisson cru à la mode."

"That's ridiculous," said Johnnie, getting up from the table.

"Where are you going?" asked Blackbeard.

"We're leaving!" said Anne. "This place is for the birds."

"This place is really something," said Johnnie, looking around the restaurant. "I feel like I'm in a pirate ship. See the antique guns on the wall?"

Anne didn't say anything. Johnnie noticed that she was frowning. "What's the matter?" he asked.

"I don't like the way that bird is looking at me," said Anne, pointing to a huge parrot in a cage.

"He must like you, just like I do," said Johnnie, smiling.

"I'm not so sure," said Anne. "He looks dangerous to me."

"Don't worry. He can't do anything. He's just a dumb bird."

a *Answer the following questions about the story.*

 1. Where did Anne and Johnnie go for dinner last night?
 2. Did they have reservations?
 3. Why didn't they like the table the hostess gave them?
 4. Why did they decide to sit at that table, anyway?
 5. Who's Blackbeard? Describe him.
 6. Why didn't Anne and Johnnie understand the menu?
 7. What did Blackbeard recommend?
 8. Why did Johnnie feel like he was in a pirate ship?
 9. Why did Anne feel uncomfortable? Was it because of Blackbeard?
10. What did Johnnie say about the parrot?
11. Do you think the parrot was dangerous?
12. What did Blackbeard say when he served Anne and Johnnie their dinner?
13. Why were Anne and Johnnie surprised when they saw the fish?
14. What happened then? What did they do?

b *Answer the following questions about yourself.*

1. Do you like to eat out?
2. Have you ever been to a seafood restaurant?
3. Have you ever eaten raw fish? raw meat?
4. Would you like to have dinner at Captain Morgan's?
5. Can you recommend a good restaurant? Why is it good?
6. What is the most important thing in a restaurant—the food, the service, or the atmosphere?

c *Make sentences using the present perfect with **already**.*

Example: Open the window!
       I've already opened the window.

1. Go to the market!	5. Clean the windows!	9. Close the gate!
2. Buy some eggs!	6. Feed the dog!	10. Lock the door!
3. Make some coffee!	7. Take out the trash!	11. Find the telephone book!
4. Wash the dishes!	8. Sweep the sidewalk!	12. Call the police!

d *Answer the following questions using the present perfect with **just**.*

Examples: Is Gloria cleaning the bedroom?
       No, she's just cleaned the bedroom.

       Are Mr. and Mrs. Bascomb reading the newspaper?
       No, they've just read the newspaper.

1. Are Sam and Mabel having dinner?	6. Is Barbara buying a new dress?
2. Are they feeding the dog?	7. Is she paying the salesgirl?
3. Is Linda taking a shower?	8. Is Barney repairing his car?
4. Is Jimmy calling Albert?	9. Are the girls cleaning their room?
5. Are they doing their homework?	10. Are they making their beds?

e   *Look at the pictures and make a sentence for each one using the present perfect with* **just.**

Anne and Johnnie have
just met each other.

Mabel _____

Peter _____

Mr. and Mrs. Bascomb _____

Barbara _____

Barney _____

Mr. and Mrs. Golo _____

Otis _____

f *Complete the following sentences using the simple past or the present perfect.*

Examples: Miss Hackey (be) _*has been*_ in town for a few days.

She (arrive) _*arrived*_ at the Plaza Hotel Friday morning.

1. Nancy (study) _____ French since she was in high school.

2. She (visit) _____ Paris last summer.

3. Up to now, we (spend) _____ very little money on furniture.

4. We (buy) _____ a small table a few weeks ago for fifty dollars.

5. I (have) _____ some free time last night, so I (go) _____ to a movie.

6. I (see) _____ a lot of movies recently.

7. Yesterday Bob (invite) _____ Linda to a party and she (accept) _____ .

8. She (be) _____ to three parties this month.

9. We (know) _____ Linda for a long time.

10. She looks much better since she (cut) _____ her hair.

g *Find out what the other students in your class have done or haven't done so far today/this week/this month. Here are some suggestions. Add your own ideas.*

Today: read the newspaper, open your mail, make the bed, eat lunch, see your friends, etc.

STUDENT A: **Have you read the newspaper today?**
STUDENT B: **Yes, I have. I read the newspaper this morning.**
       OR **No, I haven't. I'm going to read the newspaper tonight.**

This week: go to the market, do your laundry, clean your house, write a letter, see a movie, etc.

This month: have a haircut, pay your bills, go to the bank, take a trip, meet any interesting people, etc.

h *Add question tags to the following sentences.*

Examples: Gloria is out of town.   You haven't seen her.
Gloria is out of town, isn't she?   **You haven't seen her, have you?**

1. Barbara has gone to the park.
2. She didn't take the bus.
3. She got a ride with Tino.
4. They're going to have a picnic.
5. They aren't going to play tennis.
6. Maria will be there.
7. She likes picnics.
8. Peter can't go to the picnic.
9. He has to work.
10. He doesn't have much free time.
11. It's supposed to be sunny today.
12. You don't think it will rain.

i   *Answer the following questions about yourself.*

1. Do you like the weather we're having today? Is this your favorite time of year?
2. Do you think today is a good day for a picnic?
3. Do you think it's more fun to have a picnic or eat in a restaurant?
4. Where did you have lunch yesterday?
5. What were you doing an hour ago? What were you doing at this time yesterday?
6. How long have you studied English? Have you studied any other languages?
7. How many books have you read this year? Which one was the best?
8. How many times have you been to the library this month? How far is the library from your home?
9. When was the last time you bought something in a department store? What was it?
10. How much do you think prices will go up in the next twelve months? How much do you think a loaf of bread will cost in the year 2000?

ONE STEP FURTHER

Anne met Johnnie at the bookstore the other day. In Wickam City it's easy to meet people and make friends.
1. Is it easy or difficult to meet people where you live?
2. Where and how do people usually meet?
3. Do you think it's OK for a girl to go out with a boy she has just met? Why or why not?
4. Describe a typical date in your country.

SKETCH

Select one student to play the part of Anne. Select another student to play the part of Johnnie.
Situation: Anne and Johnnie meet for the first time in Johnnie's bookstore. He asks her for a date.

Select one student to be a waiter in a restaurant. Select another student to be a customer.
Situation: the waiter shows the customer to a table and brings him the menu. Later he accidentally spills soup on the customer. The customer is very angry.

COMPOSITION

1. Describe how you met an important person in your life. When and where did it happen? What were the circumstances?
2. How do people meet and make friends in your country?
3. Describe a typical date in your country. Where do people go? What do they do?
4. Describe an enjoyable dinner you had recently. Who were you with? What was special about the evening? What did you have for dinner?

VOCABULARY

adventure	deep	mail (n.)	postman	speciality
alive	deliver	makeup		
ambition		motion	raw	travel agency
	exotic		receive	
cage		next (adv.)	ridiculous	yet
calmly	fresh			
cookbook		parrot	seafood	
	live (adj.)	pick up	second (n.)	
		pirate	ship	

EXPRESSIONS

How's everything?   This place is really something.   right now
What's happened?   This place is for the birds.   a flat tire
What's the matter?   It's supposed to be out of this world.
Are you serious?   They have some friends in common.

PRONUNCIATION

v

vase	driver	serve
very	travel	have
visit	evening	leave
never	movie	save

She gave me a very expensive vase.
We've never visited the University.

f

for	often	leaf	enough
fun	defend	half	philosophy
fast	laughing	safe	
free	telephone	life	

The friendly philosopher often laughs at his wife.
She found a knife and fork on the shelf.

My friend never leaves the office before half past five.
He often drives very fast.

INFINITIVE OF PURPOSE

She's going to the post office.	

She's going	to get a package.	
	to buy some stamps.	
	to send some letters.	

She's going to the post office	to get a package.
	to buy some stamps.
	to send some letters.

PAST SIMPLE

He She I You We They	took a shower ate breakfast called Maria	a few minutes ago.

PRESENT PERFECT with JUST

He She	's (has)		taken a shower.
I You We They	've (have)	just	eaten breakfast. called Maria.

PRESENT PERFECT with ALREADY
Affirmative

He She	's (has)		met Peter.
I You We They	've (have)	already	talked to him. seen his car.

PRESENT PERFECT with YET
Negative

He She	hasn't (has not)	met Peter	
I You We They	haven't (have not)	talked to him seen his car	yet.

PRESENT PERFECT with YET
Interrogative

Has	he she	met Peter	
Have	I you we they	talked to him seen his car	yet?

Short Answers

Yes,	he she	has.
	I you we they	have.

No,	he she	hasn't.
	I you we they	haven't.

CHAPTER TWELVE

Review

On his way home from school, Jimmy Brown often stops at Brady's Newsstand on Main Street. Jimmy loves to look at magazines, and Brady's has the best selection in town. Sometimes Jimmy spends the whole afternoon reading about sports, movies, and pop music. Mr. Brady, the owner of the newsstand, is a very kind man. He doesn't mind if Jimmy looks at the magazines, as long as he puts them back in the right place.

At the moment, Jimmy is reading an article about famous actors of the silent era. Mr. Brady looks over Jimmy's shoulder and smiles. "We had a lot of great actors in those days," he says. "But if you ask me, Charlie Chaplin was the greatest."

"I've never seen any of his pictures," says Jimmy. "What's so great about him?"

"He was a master of comedy," says Mr. Brady. "Charlie Chaplin was one of the funniest men who ever lived."

"He looks funny in this photograph," says Jimmy. "Did he always dress like a bum?"

"Yeah, in most of his pictures he wore an old coat and baggy pants. Everyone called him the little tramp."

"I don't think I'd like to be a tramp," says Jimmy. "But I would like to travel and have adventures, like Charlie Chaplin did."

"There's plenty of time for that," says Mr. Brady. "Hey kid, will you watch the stand for a minute? I'm going across the street to get a cup of coffee."

"Sure, Mr. Brady. I'll be happy to."

As Jimmy is looking at magazines, he hears the roar of a motorcycle. He turns around and sees a gray-haired woman on a huge, black Honda. She jumps off the bike and takes a magazine off the rack.

"Where's Mr. Brady?" she asks.

"He went across the street. He'll be back soon."

"I can't wait," says the woman. "I'm in a hurry."

"Is there something you want to buy?" asks Jimmy.

"Yes, I want to get this magazine," she says.

"You can pay me. I'll give him the money."

The woman observes Jimmy carefully. "You look like an honest boy," she says. "I guess I can trust you." She takes out two dollars and hands the money to Jimmy. Then she jumps on her motorcycle and takes off. "Make sure he gets it," she yells, roaring down the street.

"Don't worry," says Jimmy.

A minute later, Mr. Brady comes back holding a cup of coffee. "Thanks for watching the store, kid."

"Sure, anytime, Mr. Brady. Oh, I sold a magazine while you were gone. Here's the money."

"Good kid," says Mr. Brady. He puts the money in the cash register and sits down in his chair. Jimmy watches Mr. Brady as he drinks his coffee. His hands shake a little and he gets some coffee on his shirt. "Darn it," he says. "I have to be more careful." He takes out a handkerchief and starts cleaning his shirt. Jimmy notices the wrinkles on Mr. Brady's hands, and the lines on his face. He looks at his snow-white hair.

"Mr. Brady," says Jimmy, "can I ask you something?"

"Sure, kid."

"What was it like when you were young?"

Mr. Brady finishes his coffee and throws the cup in the trash.

"You really want to know?"

Jimmy nods his head.

"Well, of course, everything was different then. Music, clothes, entertainment . . . "

"What was the music like?" asks Jimmy.

"It was terrific. When I was young, we listened to Big Band Music by Glenn Miller and Duke Ellington. You have your rock 'n' roll, which is OK, but the music we had was much more romantic. We liked to dance cheek-to-cheek."

"Were you a good dancer, Mr. Brady?"

"I don't like to brag, kid, but I was one of the best. All the girls loved to dance with me. I was the king of the Starlight Ballroom."

"The Starlight Ballroom? Where's that?"

"They closed it down twenty years ago," says Mr. Brady, sadly.

"Oh, that was dumb," says Jimmy.

"I hope I can make a trip across the ocean someday," says Jimmy. "Have you ever been to a foreign country, Mr. Brady?"

"Sure, I've been all over the world. Rio, Hong Kong, Cairo . . . . I've seen everything and done it all."

"Gee, I've never been out of Wickam City," says Jimmy.

"Don't worry, you'll get your chance. You have a spirit of adventure, and that's what counts."

"Thanks, Mr. Brady. Well, I'd better go now. It's getting late."

"So long, kid."

"Bye, Mr. Brady."

"That's life," says Mr. Brady. "Times change."

"Do you think times were better then or now?" asks Jimmy.

"Well, fifty years ago life was slower and less complicated," says Mr. Brady. "We had fewer problems with noise, pollution, and crime. But some things are better now, like medicine and transportation. People live longer and travel faster nowadays. I remember it took Lindbergh thirty-three hours to fly across the Atlantic in 1927, and everybody thought it was fantastic. They gave him a hero's welcome when he landed in France. Today, you can cross the same ocean in less than four hours, and nobody thinks anything of it."

a   *Answer the following questions about the story.*

1. Why does Jimmy go to Brady's Newsstand?
2. What does Jimmy like to read about?
3. What is Mr. Brady's opinion of Charlie Chaplin?
4. How did Charlie Chaplin dress?
5. Why does Mr. Brady ask Jimmy to watch the newsstand?
6. Who arrives at the newsstand after Mr. Brady leaves?
7. What does the woman want?
8. How much money does she give Jimmy?
9. What does Jimmy do with the money?
10. What happens when Mr. Brady starts drinking his coffee?
11. What does Jimmy notice about Mr. Brady?
12. How old do you think Mr. Brady is?
13. What kind of music was popular when Mr. Brady was young?
14. Why does Mr. Brady like Big Band Music better than rock?
15. Was Mr. Brady a good dancer? Where did he like to dance?
16. What happened to the Starlight Ballroom?
17. What was life like fifty years ago according to Mr. Brady?
18. What things are better today?
19. How long did it take Lindbergh to cross the Atlantic?
20. Where did he land?
21. How long does it take to make the same trip today?
22. What does Jimmy hope to do some day?
23. Does Jimmy have a "spirit of adventure"? What about you?

b   *Mike Brady has been around for a long time and he has opinions on everything. He likes to talk about how things have changed since he was a young man. Do you agree or disagree with his comments? Why?*

1. "When I was young, there was much less crime. The streets were safer, and we never locked our doors."
2. "People are less friendly nowadays. Most people don't even know their neighbors."
3. "Kids are smarter today. They know much more than the kids of my generation."
4. "The family is less important today. People only care about their careers and making money."
5. "Life is much easier nowadays. Machines do all the work."
6. "People are healthier nowadays. They eat better and live longer."

BARBARA: Can you do me a favor, Anne?

ANNE: What is it?

BARBARA: Can you mail these letters for me?

ANNE: No, I can't. I don't have time.

c *Have similar conversations with other students.*

STUDENT A: Can you do me a favor, _____ ?

STUDENT B: What is it?

STUDENT A: Can you _____ ?

STUDENT B: Yeah, sure. I'll be happy to.
OR No, I can't. I don't have time.

Include some of these questions in your conversations.

Can you help me with my homework?
_____ return this book to the library?
_____ make me a cup of coffee?
_____ wash the dishes?
_____ clean the windows?
_____ water the plants?
_____ go to the market for me?
_____ carry this suitcase for me?
_____ loan me five dollars?

Possible affirmative answers:

Yeah.
Sure.
OK.
Of course.
No problem.
I'll be happy to.
It's a pleasure.

Possible negative answers:

No.
I'm sorry.
I can't.
Not right now.
I'm busy.
I don't have time.
I'm too tired.

d   *Make questions with **who, what,** or **where.***

Examples: Barney has gone <u>to Mom's Cafe</u>.   He's having dinner with <u>Nancy</u>.
Where has he gone?   **Who's he having dinner with?**

They like <u>the fried chicken</u>.
What do they like?

1. Jimmy often visits <u>Mr. Brady</u>.
2. Mr. Brady owns <u>a newsstand</u>.
3. The newsstand is <u>on Bond Street</u>.
4. Jimmy likes to look at <u>magazines</u>.
5. Today he's reading about <u>Charlie Chaplin</u>.

6. Charlie Chaplin was from <u>England</u>.
7. He worked in <u>Hollywood</u>.
8. He made <u>silent movies</u>.
9. He married <u>a famous actress</u>.

e   *Find the opposites and fill in the blanks.*

noisy	dumb	dark	refuse
safe	selfish	front	west
hate	cheap	sick	wrong

1. generous   *selfish*
2. healthy   _____
3. dangerous   _____
4. expensive   _____

5. right   _____
6. love   _____
7. back   _____
8. east   _____

9. smart   _____
10. accept   _____
11. quiet   _____
12. light   _____

f   *Complete the following sentences using suitable prepositions.*

Example: There's plenty ___*of*___ time ___*for*___ everything.

1. Mr. Bascomb is president _____ the City Bank.

2. He's worked _____ the bank _____ twenty years.

3. His office is _____ the first floor _____ the building.

4. The bank isn't far _____ here. You can walk there _____ five minutes.

5. I'm going _____ Mom's Cafe _____ a cup _____ coffee.

6. Barbara and Tino are getting married _____ a couple _____ weeks.

7. They're inviting all _____ their friends _____ the wedding.

8. Mike Brady has the best selection _____ magazines _____ town.

9. I had a nice conversation _____ Mr. Brady. We talked _____ airplanes.

g *Why are these people complaining? What do you think they are saying?*

When was the last time you complained about something? What were you upset about? Tell what happened.

h *Describe what is happening in the illustrations below.*

When was the last time you saw someone do a "good deed"? Have you done any good deeds recently? Do you think most people try to help others or do they just mind their own business?

i   *Complete the following sentences using a possessive adjective or a possessive pronoun.*

Example: We have _____*our*_____ ideas and they have *theirs* .

1. My typewriter is broken. Can I borrow _____?

2. We're taking the lamp because it's _____.

3. What does Anne have in _____ desk?

4. Johnnie says those magazines are _____. Give them to him.

5. The Browns are painting _____ living room.

6. I have _____ umbrella, but Linda can't find _____.

7. Jimmy's in the bathroom. He's brushing _____ teeth.

8. You forgot _____ hat. You left it in the closet.

9. That coat belongs to me. It's _____.

j   *Complete the following sentences using **someone, something, somewhere, anyone, anything,** and **anywhere.***

Examples: Albert doesn't know *anything* about sports.

Linda can't go *anywhere* tonight. She has to stay home.

Can I use your phone? I have to call *someone* .

1. I'm hungry. I want _____ to eat.

2. There isn't _____ in the refrigerator.

3. Go to Mom's Cafe. You can't find better food _____.

4. I hear footsteps. I think there's _____ in the hall.

5. The hall is empty. I don't see _____.

6. Come here. There's _____ I have to tell you.

7. This isn't a good place to talk. Let's go _____ else.

8. I can't go _____. I don't have my car keys.

9. Don't worry. I won't tell _____ that you lost your keys.

10. The keys were in the desk a little while ago. _____ took them.

11. Don't look at me. I didn't do _____.

12. Tell the truth. Did you take the keys and hide them _____?

k *Linda is shopping for a pair of jeans. Complete the conversation between Linda and the sales-man using the sentences below.*

They're a size smaller.
I like the ones with the stripes.
Well, how do they fit?
I'd like to buy a pair of jeans.
You can try them on in the dressing room.

These are much better.
What style do you like?
They're a little too big.
Can I help you?

l *Have similar conversations. One student is the salesperson in a clothing store. The other stu-dent is a customer who wants to buy a pair of jeans, a shirt, or a dress.*

m *Make short sentences showing that you disagree with the following statements.*

Examples: Mike Brady is rich. **No, he isn't.**
He doesn't have to work. **Yes, he does.**

1. Captain Morgan's is a good restaurant.
2. It isn't expensive.
3. Barbara drives to work.
4. She doesn't take the bus.
5. Jack has worked hard this year.
6. He hasn't taken a vacation.
7. The weather was good last month.
8. It didn't rain much.
9. We can go to the movies tonight.
10. We don't have to study.
11. Linda stayed home last night.
12. She didn't go out with her friends.

n *Add an explanation to each of the remarks below.*

Examples: Hurry up! *We're late.*

OR *The show starts in five minutes.*

I admire your sister. *She's a beautiful person.*

OR *She always tries to help people.*

1. He's a lucky man. _____

2. I'm worried. _____

3. Can you loan me some money? _____

4. Don't turn off the radio! _____

5. How can you eat that food? _____

6. Speak louder. _____

7. Peter can't go to work today. _____

8. I had a terrible time last night. _____

9. Diane isn't talking to her boyfriend. _____

10. Can I use your umbrella? _____

11. I don't like to take the bus. _____

12. Nobody eats at Joe's Cafe. _____

IN AMERICA

1. *There are many races and nationalities.*

2. _____

3. _____

4. _____

5. _____

6. _____

7. _____

8. _____

9. _____

o *Write an appropriate sentence for each picture from the list below.*

Television soap operas are very popular.
Some people live to work.
Baseball is the national pastime.
Coffee is the favorite drink.
Women live longer than men.

There are many races and nationalities.
Young people enjoy rock music.
The average family has two children.
People eat a lot of junk food.

p *Answer the following questions.*

1. Are there many races and nationalities in your country? Do most people speak the same language? How many people speak English in your country?
2. What is the national pastime in your country? What's your favorite pastime? Do you like sports?
3. What is junk food? Is it possible to get a hamburger and french fries in your country? Do you sometimes eat junk food?
4. Do you enjoy soap operas? Are soap operas popular in your country? What is your favorite TV program?
5. Is rock music popular in your country? Can you name any rock bands? What kind of music do you like best?
6. What is the most popular drink in your country? How much coffee do people drink? What do people drink with meals? What's your favorite drink?
7. How big is the average family in your country? How many people are there in your family? Do you think it's better to have a large family or a small family? Give reasons for your answer.
8. What is a "workaholic"? Why do some people work so hard? Do you think most people live to work or live to play?
9. Do women live longer than men in your country? Why do you think women live longer in the United States? What is necessary for a person to live a long, happy life?

q *Complete the following sentences using* ***everyone, everything, everywhere, no one, nothing,*** *and* ***nowhere.***

Examples: All the employees are having lunch. There's ____*no one*____ in the office.

I can't find my dictionary. I've looked for it *everywhere*.

Fred is bored. He has ____*nothing*____ to do.

1. The refrigerator is empty. There's _____ in it.

2. We're all broke. _____ has any money.

3. I have to find an apartment right away. I have _____ to stay.

4. If you need help, go to Dr. Pasto. He helps _____.

5. I called him last night, but there was _____ home.

6. While Mabel was sick, Sam took care of the family. He did _____.

7. Mabel is fine now. There's _____ wrong with her.

8. My uncle loves to travel. He's been _____.

9. There's _____ more exciting than New York City. It's a great place.

10. Baseball is America's favorite sport. _____ likes baseball.

11. I've never seen so many tourists. They're _____.

12. That's life. You can't have _____.

Ed and Johnnie are going for a ride in Johnnie's car.

ED: Do you mind if I turn on the radio?

JOHNNIE: Yes, I do. Don't turn it on.

r   *Have similar conversations. Student A asks for permission to do something. Student B can either give or deny permission.*

STUDENT A: Do you mind if I _____?

STUDENT B: Yes, I do. Don't _____.
             OR   No, I don't. (It's OK.) (Go ahead.)

Use the ideas below for your conversations.

1. open the window?
2. eat your sandwich?
3. read the newspaper?

4. use your comb?
5. use the mirror?
6. look at the map?

7. take off my shoes?
8. sit in the back seat?
9. play my bongos?

s   *Americans often use shortened questions in conversation. Write the complete question form after the following shortened questions.*

Examples: Working hard?   *Are you working hard?*

            Want a cup of coffee?   *Do you want a cup of coffee?*

            Heard the news?   *Have you heard the news?*

1. Having a good time? _____

2. Come here often? _____

3. Hungry? _____

4. Had lunch yet? _____

5. Ever been to Joe's Cafe? _____

6. Anything wrong? _____

7. Need some help? _____

8. Going home? _____

9. Want a ride? _____

t   *Answer the following questions about yourself.*

1. What's the first thing you do when you get up in the morning?
2. What's the last thing you do before you go to bed at night?
3. What are your plans for the weekend? Are you going to get together with any of your friends?
4. Do you ever loan things to your friends? Do you think it's a good idea to loan books, records, etc.?
5. Can you recommend an interesting movie or book? Why do you think it's good?
6. Have you ever loaned money to someone? Did you get the money back? How long did it take?
7. Have you ever borrowed money? What did you need the money for? Did you pay the money back?
8. When was the last time you forgot something? What was it?
9. When was the last time you helped someone? What did you do?

ONE STEP FURTHER

Mike Brady says that he doesn't like to brag. But he often tells people that he was a great dancer when he was a young man.
1. Do you know anyone who brags a lot? What does he or she brag about?
2. Why do some people brag so much?
3. Do you think it's OK to brag? Do you ever brag?
4. Do you like to talk about yourself?

SKETCH

Select one student to be Mr. Brady. Select another student to be Jimmy.
Situation: Jimmy asks Mr. Brady how things have changed since Mr. Brady was a young man. Use some of the ideas in the story on pages 196–198 and some of your own ideas.

Select one student to be Mr. Brady. Select another student to be a tourist.
Situation: the tourist asks Mr. Brady if he can recommend a good restaurant. Mr. Brady describes his favorite eating place. The tourist wants to know how to get there.

COMPOSITION

1. How are Americans similar to or different from people in your country? Compare work, play, family life, etc.
2. Write about the changes that are taking place in the world or in your community. Are the changes good or bad?
3. Write about a major event that has changed your life. Compare your life before and after the event.
4. Write about a good deed that you did or that someone else did. What were the circumstances?
5. Compare your home town with the town you're living in now.

VOCABULARY

article	jump off	roar (n.)	wrinkle
	jump on	roar (v.)	
baggy		rock 'n' roll	
Big Band music	kid	romantic	
bike	king		
brag		sadly	
	line	selection	
fewer		shake	
	master	shoulder	
gray-haired		snow-white	
guess (v.)	newsstand	someday	
	nowadays		
handkerchief		terrific	
hero	observe	throw	
Honda		tramp	
huge	rack	trust	
	ride (n.)		

EXPRESSIONS

He doesn't mind.
That's what counts.
Make sure he gets it.
I'll be happy to.

What's so great about him?
Nobody thinks anything of it.
We danced cheek-to-cheek.
I'd better go now.

Darn it!
That's life.
Times change.
So long, kid.

On his way home . . .
as long as
a spirit of adventure
a hero's welcome

TEST

1. This has been a wet year.
   We've had _____ rain.

   A. many   C. a few
   B. little   D. a lot of

2. Jack is lazy. He works only
   _____ hours a day.

   A. a few   C. much
   B. a lot of   D. many

3. You're going to be a good dancer.
   You just need _____ practice.

   A. much   C. a little
   B. many   D. a few

4. We don't know _____ people
   on our street.

   A. much   C. each
   B. many   D. a little

5. I can't think when there's _____
   noise.

   A. too much   C. too little
   B. too many   D. too few

6. Linda is talking to Albert _____
   the phone.

   A. in   C. at
   B. on   D. with

7. Let's have lunch _____ Mom's Cafe.

   A. for   C. at
   B. to   D. on

8. Peter is taking Maria _____ the
   movies.

   A. in   C. at
   B. for   D. to

9. Wickam City is ten miles _____ the
   ocean.

   A. to   C. for
   B. at   D. from

10. Mr. Bascomb is president _____ a
    large bank.

    A. of   C. with
    B. for   D. from

11. Peter's car is in good condition.
    He takes good care of _____.

    A. him   C. them
    B. her   D. it

12. We're having a problem. Can you help
    _____?

    A. it   C. us
    B. we   D. them

13. Where are the boys? Are _____ at
    the park?

    A. they   C. their
    B. them   D. there

14. Sam is happy _____ he has a
    good job and a nice family.

    A. although   C. so
    B. because   D. but

15. I was hungry, _____ I made a
    sandwich.

    A. although   C. so
    B. because   D. but

16. We called your house last night,
    but there was _____ home.

    A. anyone   C. no person
    B. none   D. nobody

17. The umbrella is _____ in the
    living room.

    A. somewhere   C. everywhere
    B. anywhere   D. where

18. There's _____ wrong with the
    television. It works perfectly.

    A. something   C. nothing
    B. anything   D. everything

19. You can't use that typewriter.
    It's _____

    A. broke   C. cheap
    B. broken   D. old

20. I can't talk to you now. I'm _____.

    A. lonely   C. happy
    B. bored   D. busy

21. Gloria works during the day and studies at _____.

    A. night   C. afternoon
    B. morning   D. weekend

22. Joe's Cafe is usually empty. He doesn't have many _____.

    A. customers   C. eaters
    B. buyers   D. shoppers

23. Sandy usually has cereal for _____ in the morning.

    A. snack   C. lunch
    B. breakfast   D. dinner

24. I want every apple in the box. Give me _____ of them.

    A. most   C. none
    B. some   D. all

25. Both of those boys are smart. _____ of them is dumb.

    A. None   C. All
    B. Neither   D. One

26. The students are doing _____ lessons.

    A. there   C. their
    B. yours   D. theirs

27. Those people are friends of _____.

    A. we   C. our
    B. us   D. ours

28. My dictionary is _____ than yours.

    A. good   C. better
    B. more good   D. more better

29. Mrs. Golo is a bad dancer, but her husband is even _____.

    A. worse   C. badly
    B. more worse   D. more bad

30. You look thirsty. _____ I make some lemonade?

    A. Would   C. Will
    B. Shall   D. Must

31. Nancy is very intelligent. She _____ speak several languages.

    A. can   C. will
    B. must   D. would

32. Jack is always at the library. He _____ read a lot.

    A. will   C. must
    B. can   D. would

33. Dr. Pasto is coming. He _____ be here in a few minutes.

    A. must   C. can
    B. would   D. will

34. Jimmy is seventeen. He isn't _____ to vote.

    A. so old   C. enough old
    B. very old   D. old enough

35. Mabel is _____ to make dinner.

    A. very tired   C. so tired
    B. too tired   D. tired enough

36. We always dress _____ on cold days.

    A. slowly   C. warmly
    B. poorly   D. badly

37. If you want to be successful, you have to work _____.

    A. hard   C. good
    B. hardly   D. intelligent

38. Mr. Poole walks _____ when he's in a hurry.

    A. quick   C. slow
    B. fast   D. energetic

39. The boys often _____ football in the park.

    A. play   C. are playing
    B. plays   D. were playing

40. Barbara was sitting in a cafe when she _____ Tino.

    A. meets   C. has met
    B. is meeting   D. met

41. Jack _____ dinner yet.

    A. doesn't eat   C. hasn't eaten
    B. don't eat   D. didn't eat

42. Gloria _____ some furniture last week.

    A. buy   C. pay
    B. bought D. paid

43. We _____ cards when our friends called.

    A. was playing   C. are playing
    B. were playing D. have played

44. Otis _____ at the same address since 1980.

    A. lives   C. lived
    B. is living D. has lived

45. You haven't cleaned the kitchen, _____?

    A. have you   C. haven't you
    B. you have   D. you haven't

46. Jimmy likes sports, _____?

    A. does he   C. doesn't he
    B. he does   D. he doesn't

47. Did Maria go to a movie with Peter? Yes, she _____.

    A. go   C. went
    B. did go D. did

48. Are the Browns going to buy a new TV? Yes. they _____.

    A. are   C. do
    B. buy   D. have

49. Have you seen Fred? Yes, I _____ him last week.

    A. ran over   C. looked up to
    B. ran into   D. stood up for

50. If it's too hot in here, you can _____ your jacket.

    A. turn off   C. take off
    B. get off   D. put off

CHAPTER THIRTEEN

Superlative   Go + -ing form

a

b

a Barbara and Tino got married today. They had the biggest wedding of the year. Everyone was there. Barbara wore a lovely white wedding dress. She was the prettiest girl at the wedding. And Tino was a very handsome groom. Today they were the happiest couple in Wickam City.

1. Who got married today?
2. Did they have a big wedding?
3. Who was the prettiest girl at the wedding?
4. What did she wear?
5. Were Barbara and Tino very happy today?

b Sam Brown is the best shoe repairman in Wickam City. His prices are the lowest and his service is the fastest. People always compliment Sam on his fine work. In fact, Sam gets the most compliments and the fewest complaints of any shoe repairman in town.

1. Who is the best shoe repairman in Wickam City?
2. Does anyone have lower prices than Sam?
3. Does anyone have faster service?
4. Does Sam get many compliments?
5. What about complaints?

SHORT-WORD SUPERLATIVE

Sam is the nicest shoe repairman in town.
_____ fastest _____.
_____ busiest _____.
_____ friendliest _____.

c *Make sentences using the superlative form.*

Examples: Barbara and Tino/happy couple/Wickam City
Barbara and Tino are the happiest couple in Wickam City.

Sam/fast shoe repairman/town
Sam is the fastest shoe repairman in town.

Slim Skinner/thin boy/his school
Slim Skinner is the thinnest boy in his school.

1. Fred/lazy man/town
2. Mrs. Watkins/old woman/Wickam City
3. Linda and Jane/smart girls/their class
4. Mr. and Mrs. Bascomb/rich couple/town
5. Mr. Twaddle/short man/Wickam City
6. Alaska/big state/the United States
7. Mount Everest/high mountain/the world
8. The Nile/long river/the world
9. The Sears Tower/tall building/the world

SALESMAN: Can I help you, ma'am?

MRS. BROWN: Yes. I'm looking for a bright
               summer dress.

SALESMAN: How about this one?

MRS. BROWN: It isn't very bright.

SALESMAN: It's the brightest dress we have.

MRS. BROWN: It looks expensive.

SALESMAN: It's the cheapest dress in the store.

MRS. BROWN: Have you got it in a larger size?

SALESMAN: It's the largest dress they make.

MRS. BROWN: OK. I'll take it.

·Anne·
28 years old
5'5" tall, 108 lbs.

·Barbara·
24 years old
5'4" tall, 110 lbs.

·Maria·
27 years old
5'7" tall, 120 lbs.

d   *Ask and answer questions about the three women. Use the superlative form.*

Example: friendly
Student A: **Which one is the friendliest?**
Student B: **Maria is.**
Student C: **You're right.**   OR   **You're wrong. Barbara is the friendliest.**

1. tall   4. thin   7. busy
2. old   5. smart   8. short
3. pretty   6. young   9. heavy

e   *Answer the following questions as indicated.*

Examples: Is Mr. Bascomb very rich? *He's the richest man I've ever met.*

Is Barbara very pretty? *She's the prettiest woman I've ever met.*

1. Is Tino very strong? _____

2. Is Dr. Pasto very smart? _____

3. Is Mabel very friendly? _____

4. Is Sam very nice? _____

5. Is Fred very lazy? _____

6. Is Mrs. Hamby very fat? _____

7. Is Mr. Twaddle very short? _____

8. Is Barbara very happy? _____

9. Is Mr. Bascomb very busy? _____

a

a   Mr. Bascomb, Dr. Pasto, and Mayor Connors are three of the most important men in Wickam City. Mayor Connors is the most powerful of the three. As the head of city government, he makes decisions that affect the lives of everyone in Wickam City. Frank Connors has already served four terms as mayor and plans to retire at the end of this year.

Dr. Pasto is the most intelligent and most sophisticated of the three men. He knows a lot about the world from personal experience, while the other two men have never lived outside of Wickam City.

Mr. Bascomb is the most ambitious of the three men. He is president of the biggest bank in town, and would like to be the next mayor of Wickam City. He wants to be mayor so he can bring more business to the city. He thinks that only the mayor has enough power and influence to do it.

1. Who are three of the most important men in Wickam City?
2. Who is the most powerful of the three? Why?
3. Is he going to serve another term as mayor?
4. Who is the most intelligent of the three?
5. Is he also the most sophisticated? Why?
6. Who is the most ambitious of the three men?
7. Why does Mr. Bascomb want to be the next mayor of Wickam City?

LONG-WORD SUPERLATIVE

Dr. Pasto is the most sophisticated man in Wickam City.
_____ intelligent _____.
_____ interesting_____.
_____ unusual _____.

b   *Make sentences using the superlative form.*

Examples: Mr. Bascomb/ambitious man/town
             Mr. Bascomb is the most ambitious man in town.

             Paris/beautiful city/world
             Paris is the most beautiful city in the world.

1. Mayor Connors/powerful man/Wickam City
2. Ula Hackey/famous person/Wickam City
3. Nancy/adventurous woman/Wickam City
4. Jimmy/intelligent boy/his class
5. Mabel/energetic person/her family
6. Sam/popular man/town
7. Jack/dangerous driver/town
8. Mr. Bascomb/successful man/town
9. New York/important city/the United States

Suzy Suzuki, star reporter for the *Wickam Daily News,* is asking Jack some questions about Dr. Pasto. She is going to write a feature story on him for the Sunday edition of the paper.

SUZY: How long have you known Dr. Pasto?

JACK: About five years.

SUZY: What's the first thing about him that impresses you?

JACK: His intelligence. He's the most intelligent man I've ever met.

SUZY: He's an expert on anthropology, isn't he?

JACK: Yes, in fact, he's one of the most respected men in his profession. He's written several books about primitive societies.

SUZY: Is it true that he once lived with the dangerous Yahyah tribe on the Passion Islands?

JACK: That's right. He even went hunting and fishing with them.

SUZY: He's quite adventurous, isn't he?

JACK: No doubt about it. He's the most adventurous man I've ever known.

SUZY: And the most impressive, it seems. Now I'd like to talk to Dr. Pasto himself. Do you know where I can find him?

JACK: Yes, he's probably at home chasing butterflies right now.

c   *Complete the following sentences.*

Examples: Mr. Bascomb is the (rich) _*richest*_ man in town.

Sam is the (popular) _*most popular*_ man in town.

1. Tino is the (strong) _____ man I've ever met.

2. Dr. Pasto has the (beautiful) _____ house I've ever seen.

3. City Bank is the (successful) _____ bank in Wickam City.

4. Mr. Bascomb is the (busy) _____ man I've ever known.

5. He's the (ambitious) _____ man in town.

6. Mrs. Golo is the (bad) _____ dancer I've ever seen.

7. She has the (ugly) _____ cat in the neighborhood.

8. Simon is the (unusual) _____ person I've ever met.

9. Linda is the (good) _____ student in her class.

10. Otis is the (original) _____ artist in Wickman City.

11. Los Angeles is the (big) _____ city in California.

12. English is the (important) _____ language in the world.

d   *Answer the following questions as indicated.*

Examples: Does Dr. Pasto like to fish?
Yes, he goes fishing all the time.

Do Mr. and Mrs. Bascomb like to shop?
Yes, they go shopping all the time.

1. Does Peter like to swim?
2. Do Barbara and Tino like to ski?
3. Does Nancy like to sail?
4. Does she like to fly?
5. Does Peter like to travel?
6. Do Sam and Jimmy like to fish?
7. Does Dr. Pasto like to hunt?
8. Does Barbara like to shop?
9. Do Otis and Gloria like to dance?

Jimmy Brown plays basketball for the Tigers. He is captain of the team. Some of the boys are taller than Jimmy, but he is the most valuable player. He is the quickest and he scores the most points. All the boys like Jimmy; he is the most popular player on the team. He is also the most competitive; he hates to lose.

Right now, the Tigers are practicing for today's big game. They need a lot of practice. They have won only two games this year, and they have lost nine. However, last year the Tigers were even worse than this year. They didn't win any games. They were the worst team in the league. In a few minutes, the Tigers will play the Wildcats. The Wildcats are bigger and stronger than the Tigers. And they have a better coach. They will probably win the game.

a *Answer the following questions about the story.*

1. What team does Jimmy play for?
2. Is he the tallest player on the team?
3. Why is Jimmy the most valuable player?
4. Is Jimmy very popular?
5. Is he a very competitive player?
6. What are the Tigers doing now?
7. Why do they need so much practice?
8. Were the Tigers a bad team last year?
9. Who will the Tigers play today?
10. Which team is bigger and stronger?
11. Which team has a better coach?
12. Which team will probably win the game?

b *Fill in the missing words.*

soft *softer* *softest*   pretty *prettier* *prettiest*

expensive *more expensive* *most expensive*

1. weak _____ _____

2. thin _____ _____

3. difficult _____ _____

4. smart _____ _____

5. heavy _____ _____

6. original _____ _____

7. good _____ _____

8. bad _____ _____

9. happy _____ _____

c *Make sentences using the superlative form.*

Examples: Mr. Bascomb is more ambitious than anyone else in Wickam City.
           He's the <u>most ambitious</u> man in town.

           Mabel is very friendly and talks to everyone she meets.
           She's the <u>friendliest</u> person in town.

1. Dr. Pasto is more sophisticated than anyone I've ever met.
2. Nancy has more energy than anyone I've ever known.
3. Tino has a lot of friends, a good job, and a beautiful wife.
4. Fred never works.
5. Mrs. Watkins is 112 years old.
6. Mr. Stilt is eight feet tall.
7. Mrs. Hamby weighs 300 pounds.
8. Mr. Bascomb has more money than anyone else in Wickam City.
9. Sam has more friends than anyone else in Wickam City.

TRANSPORTATION

1. Los Angeles
2. Paris
3. Peking
4. San Francisco
5. Rio de Janeiro
6. Rome
7. New York
8. Venice
9. Jaipur

d *Describe the different means of transportation using the superlative form of these adjectives: fast, slow, safe, cheap, expensive, popular, enjoyable, famous, exciting, comfortable. Use the adjective you think is the most appropriate for each kind of transportation.*

Example 1: Los Angeles
       In Los Angeles, the most popular means of transportation is the car.

Example 2: Paris
       In Paris, the fastest means of transportation is the Metro.

3. Peking	6. Rome	8. Venice
4. San Francisco	7. New York	9. Jaipur
5. Rio de Janeiro		

e *Write sentences using **too much** and **too many**.*

Examples: cars *There are too many cars in this city.*

traffic *There's too much traffic in this city.*

1. buses _____

2. noise _____

3. people _____

4. industry _____

5. factories _____

6. pollution _____

7. crime _____

8. robbers _____

9. tourists _____

f *Complete the following sentences as indicated.*

Examples: He's never eaten Chinese food, but she *has*.
They had a good time last night, but we *didn't*.

1. She likes to work, but he _____.
2. You don't think money is important, but I _____.
3. They can attend the meeting tomorrow, but we _____.
4. He won't help us, but she _____.
5. I'm busy most of the time, but you _____.
6. We haven't seen the new hospital yet, but they _____.
7. She was at home last night, but he _____.
8. You didn't enjoy the concert, but I _____.
9. They've eaten dinner, but we _____.

g *Answer the following questions about your country.*

1. What is the largest river in your country?
2. What is the highest mountain in your country?
3. What is the biggest lake in your country?
4. What is the most important city in your country?
5. What is the most important industry in your country?
6. What is the most popular sport in your country?
7. Who is the most famous athlete in your country?
8. Who is the most famous singer in your country?
9. What is the most popular dish in your country?

ONE STEP FURTHER

Jimmy is very athletic. He loves to play basketball and football.
1. What's your favorite sport?
2. What's the most popular sport in your country?
3. What's your favorite team?
4. Who's your favorite player?
5. What's your opinion of professional sports? athletes?
6. What are the benefits of playing a sport?

Barbara and Tino got married today. They had a beautiful wedding.
1. When was the last time you went to a wedding?
2. Do you enjoy weddings?
3. Describe a typical wedding in your country.
4. What's your opinion of marriage?
5. What are some of the advantages of being married? What are some of the disadvantages?
6. What do you think is necessary for a happy marriage?

SKETCH

Select one student to be Peter. Select another student to be a young woman.
Situation: Peter gets on a crowded train and sees one empty seat. He asks the young woman
   sitting in the next seat if he can sit down. She says the seat is free. Peter and the young
   woman introduce themselves. Each one asks where the other person is going.

Select one student to be Dr. Pasto. Select another student to be Suzy Suzuki.
Situation: Suzy interviews Dr. Pasto about his life as a young man. Dr. Pasto tells her about his
   foreign travels and adventures.

CONVERSATION PRACTICE

Pairs of students discuss their favorite sports, including teams and players.
Pairs of students discuss marriage and dating.

COMPOSITION

1. Write about your favorite sport.
2. Describe an unforgettable celebration or festival you attended.
3. What's your opinion of marriage? What are some of the advantages and disadvantages?
4. Describe a person who has had a strong influence in your life. What are his or her outstanding qualities? How has this person changed or influenced your life?
5. Do you know anyone who has had an adventurous life? What were some of the
   adventures?

VOCABULARY

affect (v.)	complaint	fishing	impressive	profession	term (n.)
ambitious	compliment (v.)		influence (n.)		tribe
anthropology		government	intelligence	reporter	
	doubt (n.)	groom (n.)		respected	valuable (adj.)
bright			lake	river	
	edition	head (n.)	league		
captain (n.)	end (n.)	himself		sailing	
coach (n.)	enjoyable	hunting	necessary	score (v.)	
competitive	even			society	
	exciting	impress	player	sophisticated	
			point (n.)	swimming	
	feature (adj.)		power (n.)		
			primitive		

EXPRESSIONS

no doubt about it   get married   make decisions   from personal experience   in fact

PRONUNCIATION

æ

ask	bad	factory
after	plan	fantastic
animal	fast	telegram
address	dance	mechanic

The fat man handed a telegram to the bandit.
The happy dancer had a fantastic plan.

ə

ugly	some	country
under	club	discuss
oven	young	recover
lunch	study	Monday

The summer months are lovely in the country.
Someone is coming from the truck.

Jack had some unhappy customers last Sunday.
Is someone standing in front of the bank?

SHORT-WORD COMPARATIVE + SUPERLATIVE

old strong	older stronger	oldest strongest

big fat	bigger fatter	biggest fattest

Irregular

pretty friendly	prettier friendlier	prettiest friendliest

good bad	better worse	best worst

He's the	oldest biggest friendliest best	student in his class.

LONG-WORD COMPARATIVE + SUPERLATIVE

popular elegant	more popular elegant	most popular elegant

She's the	most beautiful sophisticated	woman in town.

GO + -ING FORM

They	go	fishing hunting swimming sailing	all the time.

CHAPTER FOURTEEN

Used to

Verb + object + infinitive

Adjective + infinitive

Who/that/which

THEN   NOW

a Tino's life has changed a lot since his marriage. He used to live in a small apartment on Oak Street, but now he lives in a house with Barbara. He used to go out with his friends at night, but now he stays home with his wife. They usually watch television together or play cards. Tino used to sleep late and never got up before ten o'clock in the morning. Now he gets up at seven and drives Barbara to work. He used to have his meals at the restaurant, but now he eats at home. For better or worse, life is not the same for Tino.

1. Now that Tino is married, his life isn't the same, is it?
2. Where did Tino use to live?
3. Where does he live now?
4. What did Tino use to do at night?
5. What does he do now?
6. Did Tino use to get up early in the morning?
7. What time does he get up now?
8. Where did Tino use to eat?
9. Where does he eat now?
10. Do you think Tino's life has gotten better or worse since his marriage?

USED TO

Tino used to live in a small apartment, but he doesn't anymore.
_____ sleep late in the morning, _____.
_____ meet his friends at night, _____.
_____ eat at the restaurant, _____.

b *Make sentences with **used to** and **anymore**.*

Examples: Tino / live on Oak Street
          Tino used to live on Oak Street, but he doesn't anymore.

          We / watch television
          We used to watch television, but we don't anymore.

1. Tino / sleep late in the morning
2. Barbara / take the bus to work
3. They / like rock music
4. Fred / work at the garage
5. Mr. and Mrs. Hamby / travel a lot
6. Barney / eat at Joe's Cafe
7. Ula Hackey / live in Hollywood
8. She / wear expensive clothes
9. Sam and Jack / play basketball

ANNE: Hello, Barbara. What are you making?

BARBARA: Lasagna. It's for our dinner tonight.

ANNE: Oh really? You never used to make Italian food.

BARBARA: Things are different now that I'm married. Besides, it's fun to cook.

ANNE: What else is new in your life?

BARBARA: Well, I used to take the bus to work, but now I get a ride with Tino.

ANNE: Is Tino a good driver?

BARBARA: I think so. He used to drive very fast, but he's more careful now. There are a lot of children in this neighborhood, you know.

ANNE: Do you and Tino plan to have many children?

BARBARA: Only two. It's expensive to have a big family nowadays.

ANNE: You're right. Well, I have to go now. Give my regards to Tino when you see him.

BARBARA: I'll be glad to. Goodbye, Anne.

USED TO: NEGATIVE

Barbara never used to make Italian food.
_____ cook for two people.
_____ go to the market every day.
_____ get a ride to work.

c   *Make sentences as indicated.*

Examples: Barbara gets a ride to work now.
           Oh really? She never used to get a ride to work.

           The children walk home from school now.
           Oh really? They never used to walk home from school.

1. Barbara makes Italian food now.
2. She drinks tea now.
3. Tino gets up at seven o'clock now.
4. He eats at home now.
5. Mr. Poole wears glasses now.
6. He smokes a pipe now.
7. Mr. and Mrs. Hamby take the bus now.
8. They save their money now.
9. They listen to classical music now.

ADJECTIVE + INFINITIVE

It's fun to cook.   It's expensive to have a big family.
_____ to go out.   _____ to eat out every night.
_____ to travel.   _____ to live in New York.
_____ to learn English.   _____ to call long distance.

d   *Complete the following sentences.*

Examples: It's fun _____
           It's fun to cook. (to play cards, to dance, etc.)

           It's important _____
           It's important to be on time. (to eat well, to exercise, etc.)

1. It's easy _____
2. It's difficult _____
3. It's good _____
4. It's bad _____
5. It's smart _____
6. It's stupid _____
7. It's important _____
8. It's expensive _____
9. It's dangerous _____

NICK: What's the matter, Fred? You look bored.

FRED: I *am* bored. I don't have anything to do.

NICK: Why don't you go to a movie?

FRED: There aren't any good movies to see.
           Besides, I don't have any money to spend.

NICK: Then read a book.

FRED: I don't have any books to read.

NICK: Well, why don't you write a letter to
           someone?

FRED: I don't have anyone to write to.

NICK: Hmm, since you don't have anything to do,
           you can repair those tires for me.

FRED: Oh, I just remembered. I have to visit my
           sick aunt. See you later, Nick.

VERB + OBJECT + INFINITIVE

Nick has some tires to repair.
_____ work to do.
_____ calls to make.
_____ customers to talk to.

e   *Change the following sentences as indicated.*

Examples: Nick has to repair some tires.
         He has some tires to repair.

         Mr. Bascomb is going to attend a meeting.
         He has a meeting to attend.

1. Linda has to do her homework.
2. She's going to write a composition.
3. Peter has to study some business reports.
4. Nancy is going to write some letters.
5. Anne is going to send a package.
6. We're going to discuss something important.
7. We have to make a decision.
8. Barney is going to tell a story.
9. Mabel has to wash some dirty clothes.

NEGATIVE

Fred doesn't have any books to read.
_____ friends to write to.
_____ money to spend.
_____ clean clothes to wear.

f   *Make negative sentences as indicated.*

Examples: Fred/books/read
         Fred doesn't have any books to read.

         We/paper/write on
         We don't have any paper to write on.

         Mrs. Hamby/knife/eat with
         Mrs. Hamby doesn't have a knife to eat with.

1. Fred/money/spend
2. He/car/drive
3. Linda/coat/wear
4. Jimmy/pen/write with
5. I/radio/listen to

6. We/magazines/look at
7. My brother/friends/write to
8. You/stove/cook on
9. The children/ball/play with

a

a   Last night a burglar broke into Dr. Pasto's house and stole most of his butterfly collection. The burglar took all the rare butterflies that were in the cabinet, while leaving the ordinary butterflies that were on the wall. As he was going out the window, the burglar made a noise and Dr. Pasto woke up. Dr. Pasto looked outside and saw the burglar, who was running across the front yard. He didn't get a good look at him, but noticed that he was wearing a black patch over one eye. Dr. Pasto picked up the phone that was next to his bed and called the police. The police captain asked for a description of the man who stole the butterflies. Dr. Pasto thought for a moment and said, "The man who broke into my house had a patch over one eye. I'm sorry, Captain, that's all I can tell you." "Don't worry," said the police captain. "I promise to find the man who took your butterflies."

1. What happened last night?
2. Which butterflies did the burglar take?
3. What happened as the burglar was leaving the house?
4. Did Dr. Pasto see the burglar?
5. What was he doing when Dr. Pasto saw him?
6. What did Dr. Pasto notice about the man?
7. Who did Dr. Pasto call?
8. Did he use the phone that was in the living room?
9. What did the police captain ask for?
10. What did Dr. Pasto say about the man who broke into his house?
11. What did the police captain promise to do?

THE RELATIVE PRONOUN <u>THAT</u>

He picked up the phone that was in the bedroom.
_____ that was next to his bed.
_____ that was on the table.
_____ that was by the window.

b   *Combine the following sentences using the relative pronoun that.*

Examples: Dr. Pasto picked up the phone. It was next to his bed.
Dr. Pasto picked up the phone <u>that</u> was next to his bed.

The burglar took the butterflies. They were in the cabinet.
The burglar took the butterflies <u>that</u> were in the cabinet.

1. He left the ordinary butterflies. They were on the wall.
2. I painted the table. It was in the garage.
3. We looked at the magazines. They were on the table.
4. She picked up the newspaper. It was on the floor.
5. He signed the forms. They were on his desk.
6. They read the telegram. It arrived this morning.
7. I took the apples. They were in the bag.
8. She wore the dress. It belonged to her mother.
9. He bought the suit. It was on sale.

BARNEY: What do you think about the butterfly theft?

FRED: I don't understand it. Butterflies are easy to catch. Anyone who steals them must be crazy.

BARNEY: Not necessarily. Dr. Pasto had some butterflies that were very valuable.

FRED: How much do you think his collection is worth?

BARNEY: It's hard to say. Perhaps five thousand dollars for the whole collection.

FRED: Do you think the burglar will try to sell the butterflies?

BARNEY: Yes, but not in Wickam City. He's probably gone to a large city to sell them.

FRED: Wait a minute. The burglar was wearing a black patch, wasn't he?

BARNEY: That's right. Why?

FRED: I used to know a man who wore a black patch. Maybe he's the man who took the butterflies.

BARNEY: I doubt it. The police found the patch the burglar was wearing. It was a disguise.

FRED: Well, he must be very clever. I hope the police catch him.

THE RELATIVE PRONOUN <u>WHO</u>

The police are looking for the man who robbed Dr. Pasto.

_____ who broke into his house.
_____ who opened his cabinet.
_____ who stole his butterflies.

c   _Combine the following pairs of sentences using the relative pronoun **who**._

Examples: Dr. Pasto saw the man. He took the butterflies.
            Dr. Pasto saw the man <u>who</u> took the butterflies.

            I know the girls. They work at the library.
            I know the girls <u>who</u> work at the library.

1. We know the woman. She lives across the street.
2. She kissed the man. He found her keys.
3. They talked to the policeman. He was standing on the corner.
4. I watched the children. They were playing in the park.
5. We heard the woman. She was singing in the shower.
6. They helped the man. He was looking for a job.
7. He thanked the people. They took care of his dog.
8. I met the girl. She worked at the bank.
9. We admire the boys. They play on the football team.

d   _Combine the following pairs of sentences using the relative pronouns **who and that**._

Examples: That's the man. He stole the butterflies.
            That's the man <u>who</u> stole the butterflies.

            Here's the patch. It belonged to the thief.
            Here's the patch <u>that</u> belonged to the thief.

1. That's the woman. She lives across the street.
2. Those are the men. They work at the post office.
3. Here are the letters. They came this morning.
4. This is the book. It belonged to my father.
5. There's the typewriter. It was in your office.
6. Those are the boys. They helped me last night.
7. That's the girl. She lost her umbrella.
8. Here's the telegram. It arrived this afternoon.
9. There's the man. He delivered the telegram.

Yesterday the police caught
the man who stole Dr. Pasto's
butterflies. His name is
Alexander Hampton. He's a clever
thief who used to work in a
circus. For years he was
known as Alexander the Great,
Master of Disguise. He was
using one of his disguises,
a black patch, when he stole
Dr. Pasto's butterflies. The
police captured him after he
tried to sell the valuable
collection to a large museum
in San Francisco.

When Alexander went to the museum, he showed the butterflies to Sy
Polanski, the museum director. As Mr. Polanski was examining the
collection, a look of surprise came over his face. He thought the butterflies
looked very familiar. The museum director suspected that Alexander was
not the real owner of the butterflies, and decided to ask him a few
questions.

"These butterflies are very rare," he said. "Where did you get
them?"

"They belonged to my father," said Alexander, who was an
experienced liar. "He gave them to me as a present."

"I see," said Mr. Polanski. "And where did your father get them?"

"My father used to travel a lot," said Alexander. "He got those
butterflies when he was in South America."

"That's very interesting," said Mr. Polanski. He noted that most of the butterflies were African butterflies, not South American butterflies. "How much do you want for your collection?"

"Five thousand dollars," said Alexander. "A very good price for such a valuable collection."

"Yes, that sounds like a reasonable amount," said Mr. Polanski. He made out a check for five thousand dollars and handed it to Alexander, who was smiling. Alexander thanked the museum director and left the room.

Mr. Polanski immediately called the police and told them about his meeting with the butterfly thief. He gave them a full description of Alexander and said that Alexander was going to the Federal Bank to cash the check. When Alexander arrived at the bank, the police were there waiting for him. They arrested him and took off his disguise.

"How did you know it was me?" asked Alexander.

"The museum director is an old friend of Dr. Pasto's, the man you robbed," said the Captain. "He recognized the butterflies you showed him."

a   *Answer the following questions about the story.*

1. Who did the police catch yesterday?
2. Where did Alexander use to work?
3. What disguise was Alexander wearing when he stole Dr. Pasto's butterflies?
4. Who did Alexander show the butterflies to when he went to the museum?
5. Why didn't Mr. Polanski think that Alexander was the real owner of the butterflies?
6. Where did Alexander say he got the butterflies?
7. How much did he want for the collection?
8. Did Mr. Polanski give him the money in cash?
9. What did Mr. Polanski do after Alexander left the room?
10. What did the police do when Alexander arrived at the bank?

b   *Combine the following sentences as indicated.*

Examples: A woman helped me. I thanked her.

I thanked the woman who helped me.

Some boys are following us. Do you know them?

Do you know the boys who are following us?

1. A man repaired our television. We paid him.

_____

2. Some girls took your magazines. I saw them.

_____

3. A woman owns that company. We know her.

_____

4. A policeman found her handbag. She thanked him.

_____

5. Some tourists arrived at the airport. I met them.

_____

6. A pretty blonde works at the bank. Do you know her?

_____

7. A tall man was here a little while ago. Did you see him?

_____

8. Some people were talking in the hall. I heard them.

_____

c   *Make questions as indicated.*

Examples: Fred wants to wear my coat.   Linda wants to write with your pen.
          Doesn't he have a coat to wear?   **Doesn't she have a pen to write with?**

1. Susie wants to ride Marty's bicycle.
2. Mr. Poole wants to use our typewriter.
3. Nick wants to go out with Barney's girl.
4. Anne wants to practice on my guitar.
5. Albert wants to play with your football.

6. Gloria wants to wear Barbara's hat.
7. They want to cook on our stove.
8. Fred wants to drive Nick's car.
9. Nancy wants to look at your magazines.

d *Answer the following questions about yourself and the city you live in.*

1. What is your favorite kind of entertainment? Where do you go when you want to have a good time?
2. What kind of movies do you like? Are there any good movies playing now?
3. Do you like to go downtown? What's the best way to get there from your home?
4. What are some of the most important streets in this city?
5. What kind of transportation do you normally use?
6. What are the advantages of driving a car?
7. What are the advantages of taking the bus?
8. Do you have any complaints about the public transportation in this city?
9. What do you think are some of the most serious problems in this city?
10. What are some things you like about this city?

ONE STEP FURTHER

Alexander Hampton used to be a great circus performer. But it was a hard life and he decided to become a thief.
1. Do you think Alexander is very clever? Why or why not?
2. What do you think will happen to Alexander? Will he go to jail?
3. Do you think he will need any of his disguises in the future?
4. Have you ever worn a disguise?

SKETCH

Select one student to be Dr. Pasto. Select another student to be the police captain.
Situation: the police captain is asking Dr. Pasto some questions about the robbery. He needs the following information:
   a. the time of the robbery
   b. Dr. Pasto's address
   c. a description of the thief
   d. a description of the stolen property
   e. how Alexander stole the butterflies

Select one student to play Tino. Select another student to play Peter.
Situation: Peter, who is a bachelor, wants to know how Tino's life has changed now that he is married.

COMPOSITION

1. Write about an interesting day you spent at the circus, at the park, or at the zoo.
2. Describe an ideal afternoon. Where did you go? Who were you with? What did you do?
3. Describe an enjoyable evening or an unpleasant evening.
4. Have you ever lost a valuable object? What was it? How did you lose it?

VOCABULARY

amount (n.)	cash (n.)	examine	lasagna	promise (v.)	stolen (adj.)
anymore	cash (v.)	eye (n.)	liar		surprise
arrest (v.)	check (n.)			rare	suspect (v.)
	circus	familiar	necessarily	real	
bowling	crazy		note (v.)	reasonable	theft
burglar			notice (v.)	recognize	thief
	director				
cabinet	disguise (n.)		patch (n.)	South American	wake (v.)
	doubt (v.)			steal	

EXPRESSIONS

Give my regards to Tino.   I doubt it.   What's new?
I'll be glad to.   Not necessarily.   How much is it worth?

PRONUNCIATION

dź

job	pigeon	large
just	engine	message
journey	original	strange
generous	pajamas	knowledge

The average vegetarian likes orange juice.
I've just eaten a strange Japanese vegetable.
The energetic stranger began his dangerous journey.

tš

chair	teacher	lunch
cheap	statue	peach
chase	lecture	which
church	situation	catch

She had lunch with the charming French teacher.
He reached for the peach that was on the chair.
Which statue is the cheapest?

The large peaches and oranges are in the kitchen.
Did they change the subject of the lecture?
I don't have much knowledge of the Japanese culture.

USED TO   Affirmative

He She I You We They	used to	watch television every day. play basketball after school. take the bus in the morning.

Negative

He She I You We They	didn't use to never used to	get up early. drink coffee. work hard.

Interrogative

Did you	use to	walk to work?

Yes, I did.

No, I didn't.

ADJECTIVE + INFINITIVE

It's	fun easy	to sing. to dance. to play the guitar.

VERB + OBJECT + INFINITIVE

We have	places to go people to see. things to do.

Fred doesn't have	anywhere to go. anyone to see. anything to do.

Do you have	any books to read? any homework to do? a pen to write with?

Yes, I do.

No, I don't.

DEFINING RELATIVE CLAUSES   People As Subject

He's the man		owns the bookshop.
We know the woman	who/that	lives across the street.
Those are the boys		found my dog.

Things As Subject

She picked up the cards		were on the floor.
It was my umbrella	that/which	was in the car.
Here's the telegram		arrived in the morning.

DEFINING RELATIVE CLAUSES   People As Object (Contact Clauses)

The man		I used to know worked in a circus.
The people	(who/that)	you met last night are good friends of mine.
That's the girl		we saw at the park yesterday.

Things As Object (Contact Clauses)

The dress		she bought was on sale.
The paintings	(that/which)	we saw were very interesting.
That's the movie		Jimmy was talking about.

CHAPTER FIFTEEN

The same as   Comparison of adverbs
As + adjective + as   Could/should
As + adverb + as

SANDY: How do you like my new hat, Gloria?

GLORIA: It's very nice. Just like the one Maria has.

SANDY: Are you sure her hat is the same as mine?

GLORIA: Absolutely. I was with her when she got it.

SANDY: She doesn't have a blouse like this one, does she?

GLORIA: No, but I bought a blouse this morning, and it's the same as yours.

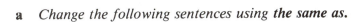

a   *Change the following sentences using* **the same as.**

Examples: Your hat is just like Maria's.
           Your hat is the same as Maria's.

           My blouse is just like yours.
           My blouse is the same as yours.

1. Our camera is just like Albert's.
2. Linda's dictionary is just like yours.
3. Tino's radio is just like Barbara's.
4. Their stove is just like mine.
5. Your lamp is just like ours.
6. Mabel's clock is just like Sam's.
7. My car is just like theirs.
8. Our refrigerator is just like Mrs. Golo's.
9. Dr. Pasto's piano is just like yours.

BARNEY: Look. Maxie Gold is going to fight the Champ tonight. I'll bet he wins.

JACK: I don't know, Barney. The Champ is very strong.

BARNEY: So is Maxie. He's as strong as the Champ.

JACK: But he isn't as clever. He doesn't have as much experience as the Champ does.

BARNEY: You're right. He hasn't had as many fights. But I still think Maxie is going to win.

JACK: Why?

BARNEY: Because the Champ is getting old. He isn't as fast as he used to be.

b   *Make sentences using **as** + adjective + **as**.*

Examples: The Champ is very strong.   So is Maxie.
He's as strong as the Champ (is).

Jimmy is very popular.   So is Linda.
She's as popular as he is.

They're very energetic.   So are we.
We're as energetic as they are.

1. Peter is very sophisticated.   So is Maria.
2. They're very intelligent.   So are we.
3. Mabel is very friendly.   So is Sam.
4. They're very generous.   So are you.
5. We're very hungry.   So is Albert.
6. He's very tired.   So am I.
7. Our friends are very lucky.   So are we.
8. Barney is very nice.   So is Nancy.
9. They're very smart.   So are you.

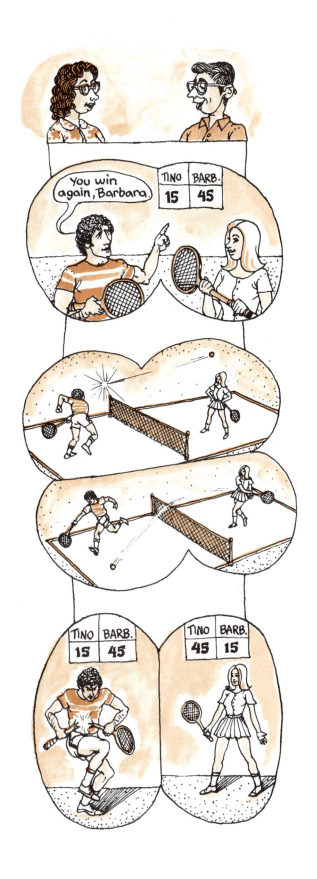

JOHNNIE: Tino plays tennis very well, doesn't he?

ANNE: So does Barbara. She plays as well as he does.

JOHNNIE: Do you really think so?

ANNE: Yes. In fact, she plays better than Tino. She wins more often than he does.

JOHNNIE: How can that be? Tino is stronger than Barbara, and he hits the ball harder.

ANNE: But he doesn't hit the ball as accurately as she does.

JOHNNIE: She probably gets more practice.

ANNE: You're right. Tino is busier than Barbara, so he can't play as often as she does.

JOHNNIE: Tino gets mad when he loses, doesn't he?

ANNE: Yes, he isn't a very good loser. Barbara accepts defeat more easily than Tino.

JOHNNIE: Why is that?

ANNE: Well, Tino takes tennis more seriously than most people. To Barbara it's just a game.

COMPARISON OF ADVERBS

They don't play as well as we do.
_____ badly _____.
_____ hard _____.
_____ fast _____.

They don't play as regularly as we do.
_____ seriously _____.
_____ competitively ___.
_____ energetically ___.

c *Complete the following sentences.*

Examples: Tino doesn't play as (good) as Barbara.
          Tino doesn't play as <u>well</u> as Barbara.

I don't walk as (slow) as you do.
I don't walk as <u>slowly</u> as you do.

        Our friends don't drive as (careful) as we do.
        Our friends don't drive as <u>carefully</u> as we do.

1. Peter doesn't read as (quick) as Maria.
2. Gloria doesn't dance as (good) as Otis.
3. They don't dress as (fashionable) as we do.
4. Mrs. Bascomb doesn't speak as (loud) as her husband.
5. We don't live as (comfortable) as they do.
6. Jimmy doesn't study as (hard) as Linda.
7. Mr. Golo doesn't eat as (slow) as his wife.
8. They don't work as (careful) as we do.
9. You don't write as (bad) as Nick.

COMPARISON OF ADVERBS

We play better than they do.
_____ worse _____.
_____ harder _____.
_____ faster _____.

We play more regularly than they do.
_____ seriously _____.
_____ competitively _____.
_____ energetically _____.

d *Complete the following sentences.*

Examples: Barbara plays (good) than Tino.
          Barbara plays <u>better</u> than Tino.

He runs (fast) than she does.
He runs <u>faster</u> than she does.

        She hits the ball (accurate) than he does.
        She hits the ball <u>more accurately</u> than he does.

1. Maria dresses (fashionable) than Nancy.
2. Mr. Bascomb works (hard) than his wife.
3. They live (expensive) than most people.
4. Anne sings (good) than I do.
5. Linda writes (careful) than Jimmy.
6. I speak (loud) than you do.
7. We work (fast) than our friends.
8. Jack drives (dangerous) than the average person.
9. Mrs. Golo dances (bad) than we do.

1

Tino could swim when he was nine years old.

Barbara could ski when she was sixteen years old.

Anne could play the guitar when she was twelve years old.

Otis could paint when he was seven years old.

Jimmy could play basketball when he was ten years old.

Nick could repair cars when he was seventeen years old.

a   *Look at the pictures from Nancy's photo album and make a sentence for each one using* **could.**

Example: one year old
   Nancy could walk when she was one year old.

INTERROGATIVE

Could she ride a motorcycle when she was in high school?
_____ sail a boat _____?
_____ play the guitar _____?
_____ speak French _____?

b *Ask and answer questions as indicated.*

Example: swim
Student A: **Could you swim when you were ten years old?**
Student B: **Yes, I could.**   OR   **No, I couldn't.**

1. ride a bicycle
2. play basketball
3. sail a boat
4. paint pictures
5. dance
6. play the piano
7. type
8. repair a flat tire
9. cook
10. make a sandwich

NEGATIVE

We couldn't go to the park yesterday because it was raining.
_____ have a picnic _____.
_____ play tennis _____.
_____ see our friends _____.

c *Make sentences using* ***couldn't.***

Examples: Barbara and Tino wanted to play tennis, but it was raining.
           They couldn't play tennis because it was raining.

           Marty wanted to go to a movie, but he didn't have any money.
           He couldn't go to a movie because he didn't have any money.

1. Susie wanted to go to the party, but she didn't have anything to wear.
2. Jimmy wanted to vote last year, but he wasn't old enough.
3. Mabel wanted to make a chocolate cake, but she didn't have any chocolate.
4. We wanted to visit the Art Museum yesterday, but it was closed.
5. Our friends wanted to take a taxi, but they didn't have enough money.
6. They wanted to call the hospital, but they didn't have the telephone number.
7. Gloria wanted to wash her hair, but she didn't have any shampoo.
8. Jack wanted to go to the football game last night, but he had to work.
9. Mrs. Golo wanted to feed the cat, but there wasn't any milk left.

DOCTOR: How are you Albert?

ALBERT: Not very well, Doctor. I feel tired all the time.

DOCTOR: You should get more sleep.

ALBERT: I get plenty of sleep. But I don't seem to have any energy.

DOCTOR: That's because you're overweight. You shouldn't eat so much.

ALBERT: You mean I should go on a diet?

DOCTOR: That's right. And you should exercise more. Take up a sport.

ALBERT: Well, I was going to play on the basketball team this year. But the coach said I was too slow.

DOCTOR: You should run more to get in shape.

ALBERT: I did a lot of running last year. But it made me very hungry, so I stopped.

DOCTOR: You shouldn't give up, Albert. Just remember, the only way to lose weight is to exercise more and eat less.

ALBERT: Okay, Doctor. I'll do my best.

d *In the pictures below, one person has a problem and the other gives advice. Write an appropriate sentence for each person.*

I have a headache.	You should get some rest.
My back is sore.	You shouldn't play with matches.
I can't sleep.	You should exercise more.
I'm out of shape.	You should take an aspirin.
I burned my finger.	You shouldn't lift heavy objects.
I'm tired.	You shouldn't drink coffee.

Yesterday Jack went to Larry Sharp's New Car Lot to buy a new car. He drove there in his old car which he planned to use as a trade-in on the new one.

"Good afternoon," said Sharp, who smiled when he saw Jack. "It looks like you need a new car."

"I sure do," said Jack. "Could you show me one that will last as long as my old car, but won't give me as much trouble?"

Sharp pointed to a very large car. "Here's one that shouldn't give you any trouble. This car will drive much better than yours and will last twice as long."

"Yes, but my car could get thirty miles to the gallon when it was new. And I think mine still doesn't use as much gas as that one does."

"Well," said Sharp, "this one probably isn't as economical as yours, but it can go much faster than yours can."

Jack thought for a moment. "I really don't want a car that goes too fast. I probably drive more dangerously than most people do."

Then Sharp pointed to a much smaller car. "That car isn't as expensive as this big one. And it's as practical as your old car ever was. It will certainly drive better than yours."

Jack walked over to the small car and looked inside. "Could you start the engine for me?" he asked.

"Of course," said Sharp. "There. Do you like the sound of this engine as well as yours?" he smiled.

"There's no comparison. Mine sounds like a sick dog and this one sounds like a happy cat. I like it."

"But," interrupted Sharp, "this one will drive more slowly than even yours, while the *big* one . . . "

"Oh," said Jack, "I like the price of this one better than the big one. Here, let me sit in the driver's seat."

Sharp sat next to Jack and grinned. "But this car is too small for a man as big as you are. I really think you should get the big car."

Jack looked at Sharp. "No. I think I prefer this one. How much will you give me for my old car in trade for this one?"

"Well," said Sharp, thinking, "your car probably isn't as valuable as you think it is. It's certainly worth more to you than it is to me. I'll give you fifty dollars for it."

Jack turned off the engine of the little car and jumped out. "What!" he said. "Only fifty dollars for my old friend? A friend I've known as long as I've lived in this city? A friend that I know as well as I know myself? A friend that has been a true friend in sickness and in health?"

Jack went over to his old car, smiled at it, and got in. "No thank you, Mr. Sharp," said Jack. "Goodbye." He started up the loud old engine.

Sharp got out of the little car and just stood there, scratching his head. He watched Jack as he drove out of the lot and down the street as fast as he could go.

a   *Answer the following questions about the story.*

1. Where did Jack go yesterday?
2. Why did he go there?
3. How many miles to a gallon did Jack get on his old car?
4. What are some of the advantages of the big car that Mr. Sharp wanted to sell Jack?
5. Why didn't Jack want a car that was too fast?
6. Did Jack like the small car that Sharp showed him?
7. How did he compare it to his own car?
8. Why did Sharp want to sell Jack the big car?
9. How much did Sharp offer to give Jack for his old car?
10. Why wasn't Jack happy with Mr. Sharp's offer?

b   *Complete the following sentences.*

Examples: He doesn't type as (accurate) __*accurately*__ as she does.

She writes (careful) __*more carefully*__ than he does.

They work (fast) __*faster*__ than we do.

1. We work (hard) _____ than our friends.

2. They don't live as (comfortable) _____ as we do.

3. You dress as (fashionable) _____ as my sister.

4. She dances (good) _____ than I do.

5. I dance (bad) _____ than anyone else in the family.

6. My mother doesn't sing as (good) _____ as my father.

7. They talk (fast) _____ than most people.

8. You listen (careful) _____ than I do.

9. I don't learn as (easy) _____ as you do.

c   *Complete the following sentences with suitable prepositions.*

Example: Mr. Bascomb has worked __*at*__ the City Bank __*for*__ twenty years.

1. Tino gets up _____ seven o'clock _____ the morning and drives Barbara

    _____ work.

2. Mr. Poole lives _____ his wife _____ a small house _____ Clark

    Street.

3. He took her _____ a nice restaurant _____ dinner last night.

4. She's expecting a letter _____ her brother who lives _____ Chicago.

5. The police captain asked Dr. Pasto _____ a description _____ the thief.

6. Dr. Pasto thought _____ a moment before he answered.

7. "The man had a patch _____ one eye," he said.

8. Miss Suzuki is going to write a story _____ Dr. Pasto _____ the Sunday

    edition _____ the *Wickam Daily News*.

9. He knows a lot _____ the world _____ personal experience.

d   *Look at the pictures and make a sentence for each one using* ***should***.

Fred should buy some new shoes.

Linda _____

Anne _____

Barney _____

Nick _____

Mrs. Golo _____

Albert _____

Mr. Bascomb _____

e   *Make sentences using **shouldn't.***

Examples: Albert eats a lot, doesn't he?   Mrs. Golo talks fast, doesn't she?
           Yes, he shouldn't eat so much.   **Yes, she shouldn't talk so fast.**

              Your friends spend a lot of money, don't they?
              Yes, they shouldn't spend so much money.

1. Sam works very hard, doesn't he?
2. Mrs. Golo worries a lot, doesn't she?
3. She drinks a lot of coffee, doesn't she?
4. Your friends smoke a lot, don't they?
5. Albert eats very fast, doesn't he?
6. Linda spends a lot of time on the phone, doesn't she?
7. Fred sleeps a lot, doesn't he?
8. He borrows a lot of money, doesn't he?
9. Jack drives very fast, doesn't he?

f   *Complete the following sentences using **so does, so do, so is, so are,** and **so am.***

Examples: Tino plays tennis well. *So does* Barbara.

           They have a lot of experience. *So do* we.

           The Champ is very strong. *So is* Maxie.

           They're crazy. *So are* you.

1. Sam is very generous. _____ Mr. Bascomb.

2. They work hard. _____ we.

3. We're saving our money. _____ Gloria.

4. She's very intelligent. _____ you.

5. I have a lot of free time. _____ Albert.

6. He likes to watch television. _____ Jimmy and Linda.

7. They're good students. _____ I.

8. We're busy this weekend. _____ they.

9. Sam has a lot of work to do. _____ Mabel.

10. He's very industrious. _____ she.

11. They live on State Street. _____ I.

12. They're usually at home on the weekend. _____ I.

READ AND PRACTICE

DR. CHANG: What's the matter?

RODNEY: I have a cold.

DR. CHANG: You should take vitamin C.

RODNEY: I've already tried that. It didn't help.

DR. CHANG: What's the matter?

MR. BASCOMB: I have insomnia.

DR. CHANG: Do you drink coffee?

MR. BASCOMB: Yes, it's my favorite drink.

DR. CHANG: Well, you shouldn't drink coffee, especially at night.

MR. BASCOMB: OK. I'll take your advice.

g   *You're at the doctor's office. One student is a patient who has a problem. The other student is the doctor who gives advice.*

h *Answer the following questions about health.*

1. What causes a headache? a stomach ache? a sunburn?
2. Do you take good care of yourself?
3. What kind of food is necessary for good health? Do you eat a lot of fruit and vegetables? What about meat? fish? milk?
4. Do you take vitamins? What is vitamin C good for?
5. Do you exercise regularly? Do you swim, jog, or play a sport?
6. How do you relax?
7. How much sleep is necessary for the average person? How many hours of sleep do you normally get?
8. Do you have a family doctor? If so, how did you find him/her?
9. Have you ever stayed in a hospital? If so, tell what happened to you.

ONE STEP FURTHER

Larry Sharp has been a car salesman for many years. He has the biggest car lot in Wickam City.

1. What's your opinion of Larry Sharp?
2. Do you think he is a good salesman? Why or why not?
3. Would you buy a car from Larry Sharp?
4. Have you ever bought something you didn't want? If so, what were the circumstances?
5. Do you think most car salesmen are honest?
6. Do you think it's important to drive a big, new car?
7. What kind of transportation do you use?
8. What's the most popular means of transportation in your country?

SKETCH

Select one student to play Jack. Select another student to play Larry Sharp.
Situation: students re-enact the story on pages 258–59 using their own words.

Select one student to be a doctor. Select another student to be a patient.
Situation: the patient is at the doctor's office because he or she feels tired. The doctor wants to know if the patient gets enough sleep, eats the right kind of food, gets enough exercise, etc.

COMPOSITION

1. What kind of people do you like? dislike? What qualities do you consider important?
2. Describe your personality. What are your good qualities? Your weaknesses?
3. What famous person would you like to meet and why?
4. What should a person do to be healthy?

VOCABULARY

absolutely	comparison	exercise (v.)	interrupt	object (n.)	similar
accept	competitively			overweight	sleep (n.)
accurately		fast (adv.)	last (v.)		sore (adj.)
again	dancing (n.)	fight (n.)	less	regularly	
as	dangerously	fight (v.)	loser	rest (n.)	thinking
	defeat (n.)		lot (n.)	running	trade (n.)
bet (v.)	diet (n.)	grin (v.)			trade-in
blouse			mad	same (pron.)	trouble (n.)
	easily	headache	myself	scratch (v.)	
champion	energetically	health		seriously	weakness
closed				sickness	
		inside			

EXPRESSIONS

Don't give up.   Get in shape.   How do you like my new hat?
I'll do my best.   I'll bet he wins. What!

PRONUNCIATION

u

good   would   put
book   could   cookie
look   should   neighborhood

I couldn't get a good look at the cook.
The good-looking football player took my cookies.

uw

who   soup   stupid
shoe   mood   student
true   noon   shampoo
food   lose   pollution

Did Mr. Poole lose his spoon yesterday afternoon?
Whose shampoo is in the living room?

The stupid cook put sugar in my soup.
Those students should be in a good mood.

COMPARISON OF ADJECTIVES AND ADVERBS

Maxie is	as	fast strong popular	as	the Champ.

My dictionary is	just like the same as	yours.

He doesn't work	as	well hard carefully	as	she does.

She works	better harder more carefully	than	he does.

COULD   Affirmative

I She They	could swim could speak French could read	when I was nine years old. as a child. before they went to school.

Negative

I He We	couldn't (could not)	go to the park have a picnic play tennis	yesterday because it was raining.

Interrogative

Could	you play the guitar he ride a motorcycle they sail a boat	last year?

Short Answers

Yes,	I he they	could.

No,	I he they	couldn't.

Polite Request

Could you open the window?

SHOULD   Affirmative

I He You	should	get up earlier. exercise more. study harder.

Negative

She We They	shouldn't (should not)	drive so fast. spend so much money. forget so easily.

Interrogative

Should	I call the hospital? we leave at five o'clock? he take his car?

Short Answers

Yes,	you we he	should.

No,	you we he	shouldn't.

CHAPTER SIXTEEN

Review

In the evening, young people in Wickam City often gather at the
Martinoli Restaurant. They eat, drink, tell stories, and have a good time.
Sometimes they talk about parties or make plans for the weekend, but
usually they just relax after a hard day of work.

One night last week Otis and Gloria were sitting at a table with
Barbara and Tino. They were making plans for a picnic when Peter came
in with Maria Miranda. Peter and Maria seemed to be arguing about
something. They sat down with their friends and ordered a large pizza.
Maria was very excited. "Have you heard the news, Otis?" she asked.

"No, what news?" said Otis.

"Banker Bascomb is running for mayor
and he plans to build a big toy factory in
City Park."

"That's not news," said Tino. "Mr.
Bascomb runs for mayor every year, and he
always loses."

"Yes, but this year he doesn't have any
opposition. The present mayor is retiring,
and Mr. Bascomb is the only candidate.
Besides, there are a lot of people who think
Wickam City needs to grow. They want to
see more industry in this town, and they like
the idea of a new toy factory."

"Okay. But they shouldn't build it in the middle of City Park," said Otis. "The park is for people, not factories. Besides, it's a great place to paint."

"Why does it have to be the park anyway?" said Barbara. "I mean, why don't they build the factory somewhere else, maybe on the edge of town?"

Peter replied, "Because the park is a very good location. You can get there easily from any part of the city. It has water and electricity, and there's plenty of room for expansion. Anyway, Mr. Bascomb has spoken to representatives of the toy company, and the only place they want to build their factory is in City Park."

"But Peter, it does seem sad," said Barbara. "What will happen to the little children who play there, and the old people who sit on the park benches and feed the pigeons?"

"What about me?" said Tino. "Where will I play tennis? The private courts are too expensive."

"And me," said Maria. "Sometimes after a hard day at the hospital I'm very tired and nervous. Then I like to relax in the park and look at the flowers and trees. They're so beautiful. I hope nothing happens to the park."

"I know what you mean, Maria," said Peter softly. "After all, we met in the park. I like the park as much as anyone else, but as a businessman, I know that Wickam City needs more industry. A new factory will provide jobs and tax money for the city. We can use the money to improve our schools and build better roads. I call that progress. What do you think, Otis?"

"I'm going to run for mayor!"

"I'm sorry, Peter" he replied, "but I can't agree. I think there are things in life that people need more than money and progress. I think we need parks and flowers and trees to be happy. Even now Wickam City has very little green space. You know it's difficult to hear a bird sing, and how can you put a price on a bird's song? I don't think it's progress to build a factory in City Park, but a step backwards."

"Why, Otis," said Gloria, "I've never seen you so serious."

"Well, Otis," said Peter, "if you really feel that way, what are you going to do about it?"

"I'm going to run for mayor," said Otis. "I'm going to oppose Mr. Bascomb and his ideas. My platform will be to save the park."

Everyone cheered and agreed that it was a wonderful idea. Even Peter was happy and ordered more lemonade for everyone.

"There's just one thing that bothers me," said Otis, scratching his head. "What's that, Otis?"

"If I become mayor, I won't have any time to spend in the park."

a   *Answer the following questions about the story.*

1. Where do young people in Wickam City often gather in the evening?
2. What do they do there?
3. Who was at the Martinoli Restaurant one night last week?
4. Why were Peter and Maria talking about Mr. Bascomb?
5. What does Mr. Bascomb plan to do?
6. Has he ever been a successful candidate for mayor?
7. Why does he have a good chance to win this year?
8. Why doesn't Otis like the idea of a toy factory in City Park?
9. Why is the park a good location for a new factory?
10. What do little children and old people like to do in the park?
11. What does Tino like to do in the park?
12. What does Maria like to do there?
13. Why does Peter think it's progress to build a new factory in City Park?
14. Why doesn't Otis agree with Peter?
15. How is Otis going to save the park?
16. What is the one thing that worries Otis?

b *Complete the following sentences using the present perfect or the past simple, whichever is more appropriate.*

Examples: Mr. Bascomb (work) *has worked* at the City Bank for twenty years.

He (become) *became* president five years ago.

1. Maria (see) _____ that movie three times.

2. She (see) _____ it again yesterday.

3. Dr. Pasto (have) _____ a very interesting life.

4. He (visit) _____ China when he (be) _____ a young man.

5. He (write) _____ several books about his travels in the past ten years.

6. Sam and Jack (be) _____ friends for a long time.

7. They (know) _____ each other since high school.

8. Jack (go) _____ to the park every day last week.

9. He (go) _____ to the park only once this week.

10. Gloria (take) _____ her car to the garage yesterday.

11. She (have) _____ a lot of trouble with it recently.

12. I (speak) _____ to her on the phone a little while ago.

c *Complete the following sentences as indicated.*

Examples: Barney has a funny story *to tell* .

Fred doesn't have any cards *to play with* .

1. Susie doesn't have a bicycle _____ .

2. Does she have a radio _____ ?

3. Sam has some letters _____ .

4. We have some dishes _____ .

5. The children don't have any money _____ .

6. Do they have any magazines _____ ?

7. I have a meeting _____ .

8. I don't have any clean clothes _____ .

d   *Look at the pictures and make a sentence for each one, using **shouldn't**.*

1

Mr. Bascomb shouldn't
speak so loudly.

2

Ula Hackey shouldn't
spend so much money.

3

Jack _____

4

Sam _____

5

Albert _____

6

Fred _____

7

Johnnie _____

8

Peter _____

e *Complete the following sentences with a suitable adjective or adverb.*

Examples: Jack laughs (easy) *more easily* than Fred.

I don't type as (slow) *slowly* as my brother.

Wickam City is (noisy) *noisier* than Colterville.

Colterville is the (peaceful) *most peaceful* town I've ever seen.

1. Mrs. Golo drives (bad) _____ than her husband.

2. She's the (bad) _____ driver I've ever seen.

3. Sam gives his time (generous) _____ than most people.

4. He's one of the (respected) _____ men in town.

5. My dog is (big) _____ and (smart) _____ than yours.

6. Barbara doesn't get mad as (easy) _____ as Tino.

7. She's a (good) _____ loser than he is.

8. Jimmy doesn't write as (careful) _____ as his sister.

9. She studies (hard) _____ than the average person.

10. Mr. Bascomb is (practical) _____ than his wife.

11. She's (friendly) _____ than he is.

12. We don't understand business as (good) _____ as they do.

f *Combine the following sentences using who.*

Examples: A girl entered the shop. She was wearing a red dress.
The girl who entered the shop was wearing a red dress.

Some people visited Dr. Pasto. They were from New York.
The people who visited Dr. Pasto were from New York.

1. A man called the office. He wanted some information.
2. A woman owned that company. She was very rich.
3. A boy found my watch. He lives across the street.
4. Some children were playing in the park. They seemed to be very happy.
5. A girl painted that picture. She's a good artist.
6. A man repaired my television. He did a good job.
7. A woman gave the party. She's a friend of mine.
8. Some people arrived late. They had the wrong address.
9. A girl sang at the party. She was very pretty.

g *Mr. Bascomb is having dinner at the Magnolia Restaurant. It's his first time at the restaurant and he doesn't like it. Look at the picture and tell what's wrong.*

h *Mr. Bascomb calls the manager to complain about the restaurant. The manager thinks there's nothing wrong. What do they say to each other? Act out the conversation between Mr. Bascomb and the manager.*

    MR. BASCOMB: This soup is terrible!

    MANAGER: What are you talking about? There's
                    nothing wrong with the soup . . .

i *The next day, Mr. Bascomb writes a letter complaining to the owner of the Magnolia Restaurant, a man named Horace Grabski. Complete Mr. Bascomb's letter.*

    Dear Mr. Grabski:

       Last night I had dinner at the Magnolia Restaurant, and it was the worst experience of my life. First of all, the food was . . .

j   *Complete the following sentences.*

Example: The woman I spoke to *gave me some good information.*
was very intelligent.

1. The man she loves _____

2. The company he works for _____

3. The city we live in _____

4. The person you told me about _____

5. The woman I met at the party _____

6. The clothes she wears _____

7. The boy Linda danced with _____

8. The restaurant you recommended _____

9. The people we live next to _____

k   *Make questions using **who**, **what**, or **where**.*

Examples: Mr. Bascomb has spoken to some businessmen from Chicago.
Who has Mr. Bascomb spoken to?

They plan to build a toy factory in City Park.
Where do they plan to build a toy factory?

A new factory will provide more jobs.
What will a new factory provide?

1. Barney has gone to the bank.
2. He's spoken to Mr. Bascomb.
3. He's asked him for a loan.
4. Jimmy was helping his father this afternoon.
5. They were working in the back yard.
6. They were repairing some old furniture.
7. Nancy went to a lecture yesterday.
8. She heard Dr. Pasto.
9. He talked about primitive societies.

l   *Answer the following questions using phrasal verbs.*

1. Are you putting aside (saving) your money to buy something special?
2. When was the last time you gave away something?
3. Do you always try on clothes before you buy them?
4. How often do you turn up late for meetings?
5. When was the last time you put off something?
6. When you have an important decision to make, do you always think it over carefully?
7. Have you ever turned down an interesting offer?
8. Have you taken up any new hobbies this year?
9. Are you looking forward to anything special this month?

JOBS

Tino Martinoli
Waiter

Anne Jones
Secretary

Richard Poole
Teacher

Maria Miranda
Doctor

Barney Field
Taxi driver

Ula Hackey
Actress

Susan Steel
Police officer

Butch Hogan
Professional wrestler

Lola Romantica
Dance teacher

m *Answer the following questions about jobs.*

1. How much do you think these people make (per day, per hour, etc.)?
2. Do you think everyone should get the same pay?
3. What are their duties?
4. What are the qualifications for these jobs? For example, to be a waiter you should have a good memory and a friendly personality.
5. Talk about the advantages and disadvantages of the different jobs. For example, a waiter gets free meals and sometimes meets interesting people in the restaurant. On the other hand, he has to be on his feet all the time.
6. Which job is the most interesting? dangerous? exciting? boring? difficult?
7. Which job is the easiest? best? worst?
8. Which job would you like to have? Why?

n *Complete the sentences about the people in the pictures, using these adjectives: tired, happy, sick, embarrassed, bored, afraid, surprised, sad, angry.*

1. Peter *is embarrassed.*   2. Mrs. Golo _____   3. Albert _____

4. Linda _____   5. Tino _____   6. Gina _____

7. Sam _____   6. Anne _____   9. Fred _____

o *Ask and answer questions about the pictures, as indicated.*

Example: Peter
Student A: **Why is Peter embarrassed?**
Student B: **He's embarrassed because he doesn't have any money.**

p *Answer the following questions about yourself.*

1. When was the last time you were in an embarrassing situation? What happened?
2. When was the last time you were surprised? What happened?
3. When was the last time you didn't feel well? What was the matter? What did you do about it? How long did it take you to get well?
4. Many people are afraid of high speeds. What scares you? Are you afraid of the dark? heights? crowded elevators?
5. What makes you happy? Do you think it's possible to be happy all the time?
6. What makes you sad? What do you do when you're feeling sad?
7. Do you work or study too hard? Are you tired today? When was the last time you had a day off?
8. When was the last time you were angry about something? What happened?
9. Are you ever bored? What do you do in your free time?

q *Write a short paragraph about a time when you were very surprised, happy, sad, angry, or afraid. What were the circumstances?*

r *Rewrite the following sentences using the adverbs indicated.*

Examples: (yet) Anne isn't here. *Anne isn't here yet.*

(still) We're waiting for her. *We're still waiting for her.*

(perhaps) She's working late. *Perhaps she's working late.*

1. (really) Maria likes her job. _____
2. (much) She works harder than most people. _____
3. (recently) We haven't seen Peter. _____
4. (maybe) He's out of town. _____
5. (very) Barbara is worried. _____
6. (anywhere) She can't find her keys. _____
7. (just) Jack has left his apartment. _____
8. (probably) He's gone to the park. _____
9. (again) I'd like to talk with you. _____
10. (here) Let's meet tomorrow. _____
11. (yet) We haven't been to the beach. _____
12. (unfortunately) The weather has been bad. _____
13. (still) Is Sandy working at the office? _____
14. (soon) I hope she'll come home. _____

✦Entertainment Guide✦

✦Cinema

"a splendid comedy"
☆ **ODEON** ☆
★★★★★★★★★★★★★
6:00 - 8:00 - 10:00 ·

"wonderfully romantic..."
Plaza
5:00 - 7:30-10:00

"Non-stop action"
Rainbow
5:30 - 7:15-9:00

✦Music

Tickets:
$14 - $12 - $10 - $5
Palace 7:30·10:30

$16.00 - $12.50 - $9.00
Music Center
·· 8:30 pm.

free admission!
Recital Hall ☆
· 8:PM ·

✦Special Events

Tickets: $35,25,20,15
Pacific Auditorium
· saturday 8:00 pm·

$15.00 - $12.50-$10.00
Wickam Stadium
show times 4:30, 7:30

$20.00 - $15.00 - $12.00
Olympic Auditorium
main event 9:30 p.m.

s   *Answer the following questions about today's entertainment in Wickam City.*
Look at the entertainment guide on page 280.

1. Where is *Dream Lover* playing?
2. Who's the star of the movie?
3. Is it a comedy or a love story?
4. What time is the last show?
5. What kind of music do the Beach Bums play?
6. Where are they performing tonight?
7. What time is their first show?
8. How much are the best seats?
9. What time is the boxing match?
10. Who is "Choo Choo" Kelly going to fight tonight?
11. How much are the cheapest seats?
12. Where's the place to go if you don't have any money?

Peter and his friends are making plans for this evening.

t   *You and your friends are trying to decide what to do tonight. Look at the entertainment guide and discuss the different possibilities. Decide (a) where to go, (b) what time you're going to go, and (c) how you're going to get there.*

u   *Complete the following dialogue using the words will, won't, can, can't, could, couldn't, should, shouldn't, would, shall, and must.*

MRS. BASCOMB: Hello, John. How was your day at the bank?

MR. BASCOMB: Very busy. I had a lot of work today.

MRS. BASCOMB: You ___*must*___ be tired. _____ you like a glass of lemonade?

MR. BASCOMB: Yes, and _____ you bring me some cookies, too?

MRS. BASCOMB: There aren't any left. I _____ make some more tomorrow.

MR. BASCOMB: Good idea. Have you seen the newspaper, dear?

MRS. BASCOMB: Yes, it's in the bedroom. _____ I get it for you?

MR. BASCOMB: No, I _____ read it later. I _____ like to look over some business reports first.

MRS. BASCOMB: But John, you _____ relax when you come home. Why don't you study those reports at the office tomorrow?

MR. BASCOMB: I _____ have enough time. I have several meetings to attend and a lot of people to see.

MRS. BASCOMB: That reminds me, did Peter come to the bank today?

MR. BASCOMB: No, he _____ come because his car was at the garage.

MRS. BASCOMB: His car is always at the garage. It _____ cost him a lot of money.

MR. BASCOMB: It does. Peter likes to drive fast and it's very bad for his car.

MRS. BASCOMB: He _____ drive so fast. Some day he _____ have another accident.

MR. BASCOMB: I'm afraid you're right. But you _____ tell Peter these things, he _____ listen.

MRS. BASCOMB: It's too bad. He's such a fine young man. And his girlfriend Maria is so attractive.

MR. BASCOMB: Yes, they're a nice couple. _____ we invite them for dinner this week?

MRS. BASCOMB: Sure. What day _____ you like to have them?

MR. BASCOMB: How about Thursday night? You _____ make some spaghetti and I _____ get the drinks.

MRS. BASCOMB: That _____ be great, John.

v *Answer the following questions about yourself.*

1. What were you doing yesterday morning at ten o'clock?
2. Where did you go last Sunday?
3. How much exercise do you get?
4. Do you plan to take up a new hobby or sport this year?
5. What are some things you like to do? Hate to do?
6. What are you going to do this weekend?
7. Where will you spend your next vacation?
8. Have you made any important decisions recently?
9. What is your greatest ambition? Why?

ONE STEP FURTHER

Mr. Bascomb wants to build a toy factory in City Park. Otis wants to keep the park as it is.
1. Who do you think is right, Mr. Bascomb or Otis?
2. Do you think it's "progress" to build a new factory in City Park? Why or why not?
3. Do you think more business means progress? Why or why not? What are your feelings about progress?
4. Where do young people get together where you live? What do they do there?
5. What are the parks like in your city? When was the last time you went to the park?

SKETCH

Select one student to be Otis. Select another student to be Mr. Bascomb.
Situation: they debate the construction of a new toy factory in City Park.

Select one student to be Peter. Select another student to be Sandy, and a third student to be the waiter in a restaurant.
Situation: Peter and Sandy have just finished their lunch and the waiter is showing Peter the bill. Peter is very embarrassed because he doesn't have any money. He asks the waiter if he can pay next week. The waiter says no. Sandy offers to help.

CONVERSATION PRACTICE

Pairs of students discuss a current issue, such as the need for growth versus protection of the environment.

COMPOSITION

1. Does growth always mean progress? What are your feelings about progress? What can we do to improve society?
2. Give your opinion on a current issue.
3. Write about a job you would like to have. What makes this job interesting? Why do you think you would be good at this job?
4. Write about an important decision you made.
5. What's the most embarrassing thing that ever happened to you?
6. What's your greatest ambition? Why?

VOCABULARY

agree
anyway
aside

bother (v.)
build

chance (n.)
character
cheer (v.)
chief (n.)
comfortably

custom

edge (n.)
electricity
embarrassed
excited
expansion

gather

improve
island

maybe
middle (n.)

native (n.)
nervous
news (n.)

offend
oppose
opposition

platform (n.)
present (adj.)
private (adj.)
progress (n.)

road

seem
someday
success

tax (n.)

wrestler

EXPRESSIONS

Have you heard the news?
He's running for mayor.

in the middle of
on the edge of

I know what you mean.
I'm looking forward to it.

after all
a step backwards

What are you talking about?
That sounds good.

first of all
Neither do I.

TEST

1. She only has _____ free time on the weekends.
   A. much
   B. a few
   C. a little
   D. any

2. He doesn't drink _____ coffee.
   A. much
   B. some
   C. a little
   D. many

3. They don't know _____ people in Florida.
   A. much
   B. some
   C. a few
   D. many

4. There are _____ magazines in the living room.
   A. any
   B. a few
   C. much
   D. a little

5. We bought _____ food today.
   A. much
   B. many
   C. a lot of
   D. plenty

6. None of those glasses are clean. _____ of them are dirty.
   A. Some
   B. All
   C. Both
   D. Many

7. I don't think there's _____ home.
   A. any person
   B. someone
   C. any people
   D. anyone

8. She has _____ in her handbag.
   A. something
   B. some thing
   C. a thing
   D. anything

9. He was late _____ he took a taxi.
   A. as
   B. so
   C. then
   D. since

10. Unfortunately, I _____ wash the dishes now.
    A. can
    B. like to
    C. have to
    D. try to

11. I think that man is a burglar. _____ I call the police?
    A. Could
    B. Will
    C. Shall
    D. Would

12. _____ you open the window, please?
    A. Could
    B. Shall
    C. Should
    D. Must

13. Mr. Bascomb works very hard. He _____ relax more.
    A. likes to
    B. would
    C. shall
    D. should

14. Barbara _____ like to play tennis tomorrow.
    A. shall
    B. would
    C. can
    D. will

15. She _____ play tennis yesterday because it was raining.
    A. won't
    B. can't
    C. couldn't
    D. shouldn't

16. Barney is very happy. He _____ like his job.
    A. should
    B. will
    C. must
    D. has to

17. Mrs. Golo is fond of her students. She's giving _____ some candy.
    A. them
    B. to them
    C. they
    D. for them

18. My sister called last week. I haven't spoken _____ since.
    A. him
    B. she
    C. her
    D. to her

19. Peter received a letter _____ France yesterday.
    A. to
    B. by
    C. of
    D. from

20. He has an apartment _____ Maple Street.
    A. at   C. in
    B. on   D. between

21. The girls are washing _____ clothes.
    A. there   C. their
    B. theirs   D. them

22. _____ some paper on the desk.
    A. It has   C. There are
    B. They're   D. There's

23. Jimmy isn't _____ to vote.
    A. very old   C. old enough
    B. enough old   D. old for

24. People respect Dr. Pasto. They _____ him because of his great knowledge.
    A. look up to   C. look up
    B. look at   D. look for

25. Sandy likes the green dress. She's _____ now.
    A. trying for it   C. trying it on
    B. trying them on   D. trying on it

26. Have you been to the post office? Yes, I _____ .
    A. did   C. go
    B. have   D. was

27. You don't like hamburgers, _____ ?
    A. you don't   C. don't you
    B. you do   D. do you

28. That's the _____ dog I've ever seen.
    A. smarter   C. more smart
    B. smartest   D. most smart

29. The living room is _____ than the kitchen.
    A. bigger   C. biggest
    B. more bigger   D. more big

30. They work in the _____ building in Wickam City.
    A. modern   C. more modern
    B. modernest   D. most modern

31. She dances as _____ as he does.
    A. good   C. well
    B. better   D. fine

32. They live _____ than we do.
    A. comfortable   C. more comfortably
    B. comfortably   D. much comfortably

33. She runs _____ than her brother.
    A. faster   C. fastest
    B. as fast   D. more fast

34. I have _____ experience than you do.
    A. as much   C. a little
    B. less   D. fewer

35. They _____ the dishes when she left.
    A. was washing   C. are washing
    B. were washing D. have washed

36. At eight o'clock last night I _____ a book.
    A. was reading   C. have read
    B. read   D. am reading

37. He was working at the office when the telegram _____ .
    A. was arriving C. has arrived
    B. arrived   D. arrives

38. Our friends _____ in town since last Monday and they are still here.
    A. are   C. will be
    B. were   D. have been

39. They _____ to the park yet.
    A. didn't go   C. haven't gone
    B. have gone   D. don't go

40. We _____ a good movie last week.
    A. saw   C. were seeing
    B. have seen   D. see

41. Has Linda finished her homework yet?

    Yes, she _____ it a little while ago.
    A. finishes   C. has finished
    B. finished   D. is finishing

42. This is the first time I _____ tennis this month.
    A. play   C. have played
    B. am playing   D. played

43. Albert has gone to the market _____ some eggs.
    A. for buying   C. for buy
    B. to buy   D. buy

44. Sam likes to _____ on the weekends.
    A. go fish   C. go fishing
    B. go to fish   D. do fishing

45. He _____ play basketball in high school.
    A. use to   C. like to
    B. used to   D. always

46. I didn't _____ like Chinese food.
    A. use to   C. used
    B. used to   D. usually

47. They don't have _____ to go.
    A. nowhere   C. any where
    B. somewhere   D. anywhere

48. She has a meeting _____.
    A. to go   C. to attend
    B. to see   D. to visit

49. We took the oranges _____ were in the refrigerator.
    A. that   C. there
    B. who   D. those

50. Do you know the man _____ lives across the street?
    A. which   C. who
    B. there   D. what

IRREGULAR VERBS

INFINITIVE	PAST TENSE	PAST PARTICIPLE	INFINITIVE	PAST TENSE	PAST PARTICIPLE
be	was	been	lay	laid	laid
become	became	become	lead	led	led
bet	bet	bet	leave	left	left
break	broke	broken	lose	lost	lost
bring	brought	brought	make	made	made
build	built	built	meet	met	met
buy	bought	bought	put	put	put
catch	caught	caught	read	read	read
come	came	come	ride	rode	ridden
cut	cut	cut	run	ran	run
do	did	done	see	saw	seen
drink	drank	drunk	sell	sold	sold
drive	drove	driven	shine	shone	shone
eat	ate	eaten	sing	sang	sung
feed	fed	fed	sit	sat	sat
feel	felt	felt	sleep	slept	slept
fight	fought	fought	speak	spoke	spoken
find	found	found	spend	spent	spent
fly	flew	flown	stand	stood	stood
forget	forgot	forgotten	steal	stole	stolen
get	got	got	swim	swam	swum
give	gave	given	take	took	taken
go	went	gone	teach	taught	taught
grow	grew	grown	tell	told	told
have	had	had	think	thought	thought
hear	heard	heard	understand	understood	understood
hide	hid	hidden	wake	woke	waked
hit	hit	hit	wear	wore	worn
hold	held	held	win	won	won
know	knew	known	write	wrote	written

VOCABULARY

This vocabulary includes all the words introduced in the text, along with the number of the page on which the word appears for the first time. Nouns are given in the singular only. Verbs are given in the infinitive form.

Parts of speech have been omitted except for words that can be used as more than one part of speech. These abbreviations are used: adj. = adjective; adv. = adverb; conj. = conjunction; interj. = interjection; n. = noun; prep. = preposition; pron. = pronoun; v. = verb.

absolutely, 249
accept, 130
accident, 117
accurately, 251
advantage, 132
adventure, 183
adventurous, 150
advertisement, 58
affect (v.), 220
affirmatively, 60
afford, 61
afterwards, 27
again, 251
age (n.), 145
aggressive, 63
ago (adv.), 110
agree, 271
air conditioning, 59
alive, 188
all (pron.), 39
almost, 132
ambition, 184
ambitious, 220
ambulance, 117
amount (n.), 242
angrily, 57
anthropology, 219
anymore, 232
anything, 43
anyway, 61
anywhere, 43
area, 127
arrest (v.), 242
article, 196
artistic, 150
aside, 276
athletic, 150
attendant, 117
attitude, 56
attractive, 150

author (n.), 47
automobile, 122
available, 58
average (adj.), 152
average-sized, 132

bacon, 8
bag (n.), 99
baggy, 196
balance (v.), 127
bandit, 101
barber (n.), 111
barn, 153
beauty, 132
become, 168
begin, 62
besides, 31
bet (v.), 250
Big Band music, 198
bike, 197
blouse, 249
blue, 17
bongos, 56
bookshop, 4
both (pron.), 39
bother (v.), 271
bowling, 231
brag, 198
break (v.), 153
breathe, 56
briefcase, 31
bright, 217
brochure, 83
broken, 61
brush (n.), 9
bucket, 9
budget, 84
build, 269
burglar, 238
burn (v.), 171

cab, 31
cabinet, 238
cafeteria, 80
cage, 188
calmly, 188
camera, 50
candidate, 133
captain (n.), 223
carpet, 59
carrot, 12
cash (n.), 242
cash (v.), 242
cash register, 13
catch (v.), 105
cause (v.), 117
ceiling, 61
cent, 5
certain, 132
champion, 250
chance (n.), 271
change (v.), 168
check (n.), 242
cheer (v.), 271
chest, 62
child, 46
childhood, 170
chocolate (n.), 43
choice (n.), 157
cinema, 110
circle, 60
circus, 241
clamp, 62
client, 95
close (adj.), 59
closed, 255
cloud (n.), 13
coach (n.), 223
collect, 4
comfortable, 150
comfortably, 286

comic book, 9
comparison, 258
competitive, 223
competitively, 252
complain, 56
complaint, 216
compliment (v.), 216
condition, 61
consider, 96
cook (v.), 21
cookbook, 180
cooking, 128
copy (n.), 111
corn, 171
cost (v.), 32
cotton (adj.), 77
cough (v.), 128
court (n.), 95
crack, 61
crazy, 239
cream, 6
crime, 133
criticize, 62
crop, 171
cry, 57
cuisine, 83
current (adj.), 133
curtain, 61

daily, 109
dance (n.), 82
dark (adj.), 61
date (n.), 63
decide, 48
decision, 151
deep, 188
defeat (n.), 251
defend, 95
deliver, 180

deposit (n.), 83
describe, 16
destroy, 171
diet (n.), 256
difficult, 56
dine, 83
dining table, 58
director, 241
disappointed, 128
discotheque, 15
disguise (n.), 239
disgusting, 56
distance, 80
doubt (n.), 221
doubt (v.), 239
dozen, 4
drink (n.), 81
drip, 61
driving (n.), 31
dumb, 63

easily, 251
east (adj.), 132
economical, 150
economics, 166
edge (n.), 270
edition, 221
election, 133
electricity, 58
elegant, 150
else, 9
embarrassed, 283
end (n.), 60
energetic, 130
energetically, 251
energy, 98
engaged, 168
engagement, 167
engine, 31
enjoyable, 225